The Playtime Boutique

50 Fast, Fun, and Easy Projects
to Sew for Your Child

Ann Poe
Kandy Schneider

CB

CONTEMPORARY BOOKS

Library of Congress Cataloging-in-Publication Data

Poe, Ann.
    The playtime boutique : 50 fast, fun, and easy projects to sew for
your child / Ann Poe and Kandy Schneider.
        p.   cm.
    ISBN 0-8442-0092-1
    1. Sewing.   2. Children's paraphernalia.   3. Soft toy making.
I. Schneider, Kandy.   II. Title.
TT715.P6397   2000
746—dc21

                                                        99-58342
                                                           CIP

For our children and grandchildren

No one has yet fully realized the wealth of sympathy, kindness,
and generosity hidden in the soul of a child. The effort of
every true education should be to unlock that treasure. . . .
Emma Goldman

One of the luckiest things that can happen to you in life
is, I think, to have a happy childhood.
Agatha Christie

Cover design by Jennifer Locke
Photography by Sharon Hoogstraten
Interior design by Mary C. Lockwood
Interior illustrations by Shauna Mooney Kawasaki

Published by Contemporary Books
A division of NTC/Contemporary Publishing Group, Inc.
4255 West Touhy Avenue, Lincolnwood (Chicago), Illinois 60712-1975 U.S.A.
Printed in Hong Kong by Midas Printing Company Ltd.
International Standard Book Number: 0-8442-0092-1

01 02 03 04 05 06 MS 19 18 17 16 15 14 13 12 11 10 9 8 7 6 5 4 3 2 1

Contents

Introduction

Children are busy every waking moment, exploring their kingdoms, savoring each new experience, and delighting in their latest discoveries. They are enchanting, creative, loving, and energetic. They grow up in a flash, but one way to treasure and enjoy these magical years is to make special projects for both of you to enjoy.

All of the projects in *The Playtime Boutique* are easy to make, even for beginning stitchers. Detailed diagrams and step-by-step instructions are included for every project. There are tips throughout to make your sewing go smoothly. Try one of the options or variations to make your project unique. Don't worry about making a mistake—most sewing errors are easily disguised. Just remember that your child will love everything you make.

As the little ones in your life grow, let them participate in decorating their rooms or making new playthings. Youngsters can help you search for a theme fabric that reflects a special interest—perhaps a fascination with jungle animals, hot air balloons, dinosaurs, or kites. Use favorite colors that have special appeal. As your work progresses, be sure to let them see and touch. It's a nice way to show young children that their opinions matter and they are special and loved.

Hints and Techniques (page 115) covers what you need to know to do the projects in this book. Take time to read this section; it's a good review of current techniques and sewing aids, especially if you haven't been sewing much lately. For example, several projects feature appliqué—an easy technique when you use paper-backed fusible adhesive. The methods used in our previous book, *Getting Ready for Baby*, apply to these projects, too. We've added more techniques, more tips, and more options, and sewing machine shortcuts are recommended throughout.

Children are blessed with creative genius. Their pretend worlds are full of dreams and fantasies, laughter and fun. These are precious years, full of magical moments. We hope the projects you make from this book will inspire your child's imagination. Such an enchanted universe deserves to be protected and treasured.

Ann Poe
Kandy Schneider

Getting Started

Sewing for children should be relaxing and fun. The projects are easy, the directions are clear, and there are plenty of step-by-step diagrams to help you along the way. So turn on your favorite radio station, play some CDs, or listen to an audio book while sewing. Use this time to unwind, clear your mind, and let go of the pressures of the day.

Getting Ready to Sew

Sewing machine—Make sure your sewing machine is in *good working condition*. Get out your manual, and clean and oil your machine as recommended. It should be serviced by a professional on a regular basis, every year or two.

Supplies—Organize your sewing paraphernalia; know what you need and where it is. Put your scissors, threads, rotary cutter, ruler, and cutting mat in a handy place. Set up your iron and ironing board. Make sure there's a new needle in your machine, then wind some extra bobbins. Once you start a project, you can use all your time for sewing without having to stop to find missing tools and materials.

Fabric preparation—Since you're sewing for a child, be sure to preshrink your fabric before cutting it. Check the project supply list to make sure you have notions, such as buttons, ribbons, and elastic, in your sewing box. These projects are quite easy to make, and you'll want all items handy so you can finish quickly.

Tools and Materials

You'll need a basic set of sewing supplies. Keep them convenient and close at hand in a sewing organizer. Plastic fishing-tackle boxes have small compartments that are just the right size for organizing machine feet and sewing notions.

Fabric—If you are planning to make several items that coordinate, buy all your fabric at the same time. First pick a theme fabric, then select coordinating fabrics. As you find the time to make each item, the perfect fabric will be waiting. Wash and iron fabric before sewing in order to preshrink it and remove excess sizing and dyes. Fabric suggestions are included for each set of projects. Remember that selvages should not be used, even in a seam allowance. Costume fabrics often require special handling. Be sure you're familiar with the hints and techniques starting on page 115 before beginning.

Needles—Keep an assortment of sizes available for both hand and machine sewing. Machine sizes 70/10 and 80/12 are the most commonly used. They dull quickly, so change needles often. You'll also need special needles for certain techniques, such as topstitching on heavy fabrics, stitching through multiple layers of fabric, or when using unique threads, such as metallic, machine embroidery, or quilting threads. Label the sections of a "tomato" pincushion to keep needles organized. Choose needle type to accommodate the thread; choose needle size to accommodate the fabric.

Paper-backed fusible adhesive—This is essential for making easy appliqués (see page 115). For easy removal of the paper backing, score it (make an X) with a straight pin.

Pins and pincushions—Fine pins with long shanks and large heads are easy to use. Glass-head pins are recommended because they can survive a hot iron without melting.

Rotary cutter, cutting mat, ruler—These tools make it easy to cut several layers of fabric at once, so strip-pieced projects like the *Courthouse Steps* quilt (page 25) can be cut and pieced in one day. The cutting blade is very sharp, so take care to keep it closed and away from small fingers.

Scissors—You'll need shears for cutting fabric, everyday scissors for cutting paper, and small embroidery scissors for trimming threads.

Seam ripper—Even the most experienced stitchers make mistakes. This little tool is essential.

Sewing machine and presser feet—Before you start, make sure your sewing machine is in good working condition. Clean and oil it as recommended in your manual. The feet you'll use most for the projects are: straight/zigzag foot, open-toed appliqué foot, overcast foot, and zipper foot. You'll also need a beading foot for the costumes in Chapter 5, Make-Believe Adventures.

Stabilizer—You'll need a stabilizer to prevent fabric from distorting during appliqué and machine embroidery (see page 115). Remember to remove it from the back of the fabric when you're finished. For the projects in this book, fusible tear-away stabilizer is also used. This is a good stabilizer for satin stitching (see page 123), though it must be removed when the stitching is completed. Hold down the embroidery and slowly remove the stabilizer, taking care to avoid ripping out stitches.

Threads—Always use the best quality threads. Inexpensive threads are too fuzzy and break easily. All threads are not alike; each has special properties of weight, thickness, tensile strength, finish, etc., so use the right thread for your task.

For the machine embroidery techniques in this book, use machine embroidery threads in the needle. These are typically made of cotton, silk, metallic, rayon polyester, or acrylic, and come in a wide variety of colors and weights. Use a fine, lightweight thread in the bobbin.

For machine quilting, use machine-quilting thread colors that match the top and bottom layers of your quilt. For details that show, use contrasting colors.

Monofilament threads are nearly invisible—smoke-colored and clear. As with any quilting threads, these threads will also add dimension and texture. For machine quilting with monofilament thread, use it in the needle and regular sewing thread in the bobbin.

notebook

Start your own reference notebook, so you can keep track of what works and what doesn't. Staple a test sample on each page, then record type of fabric, top and bobbin thread brands and colors, needles, machine settings (stitch length, stitch width, tension), stabilizer, and any other pertinent data.

A Castle in the Clouds
Little Girl's Bedroom

A young princess will live happily ever after in this enchanting bedroom. A pajama pillow holds sleepwear during the day. Charming accessories, including window valance banners, bed swag, pillow sham, dust ruffle, lampshade, and petal pillow, make a fairyland for little girls. A tiny purse for the Tooth Fairy awaits each baby tooth.

fabric recommendations

Cotton

Cotton/polyester blends

Decorator fabrics

Projects shown use fifteen coordinating fabrics.

castle quilt

The castle on this quilt invites little ones to an imaginary land full of flowers and sweet dreams. Vines and flowers embroidered on each turret add dimension to this appliqué quilt. Finished size is for twin bed 62″ × 84″ (155 cm × 210 cm).

Supplies

Fabric	Piece	Amount	Cut	Size
Quilt				
B	Sky	1⅛ yd (1 m)	1	36½″ × 36½″ (92.75 cm × 92.75 cm)
A	Ground	¾ yd (0.75 m)	1	24½″ × 36½″ (62 cm × 92.75 cm)
F	Inside border	1¾ yd (1.6 m)	2	6½″ × 62″ (16.25 cm × 157.5 cm)
			2	6½″ × 52″ (16.25 cm × 132 cm)
E	Outside border	2¼ yd (2.1 m)	2	6½″ × 74″ (16.25 cm × 188 cm)
			2	6½″ × 64″ (16.25 cm × 162.5 cm)
O	Quilt back	5 yd (2.5 m)	1	44″ × 88″ (110 cm × 223.5 cm)
			2	12″ × 88″ (30 cm × 223.5 cm)
D	Extra-wide double-fold bias tape	8½ yd (4.5 m)		
	Batting	Twin size		
Motif				
C	Castle	½ yd (0.5 m)	1	See pattern
D	Turrets	½ yd (0.5 m)	2	See pattern
E	Turret roofs	8″ × 12″ (20 cm × 30 cm)	2	See pattern
F	Door	5″ × 7″ (12.5 cm × 18 cm)	1	See pattern
F	Windows	6″ × 6″ (15 cm × 15 cm)	4	See pattern
E	Flags (background)	4″ × 12″ (10 cm × 30 cm)	2	See pattern
M	Flags (foreground)	4″ × 12″ (10 cm × 30 cm)	2	See pattern
N	Clouds	9″ × 15″ (23 cm × 37.5 cm)	3	See pattern
H	Large trees	¼ yd (0.25 m)	2	See pattern
L	Large tree trunks	4″ × 8″ (10 cm × 20 cm)	2	See pattern

Motif (continued)

I	Small tree	4" × 10" (10 cm × 25 cm)	2	See pattern
J	Large bush	7" × 8" (18 cm × 20 cm)	2	See pattern
K	Small bush	5" × 8" (12.5 cm × 20 cm)	2	See pattern
G	Path	½ yd (0.5 m)	1	See pattern

fusing order

1. Castle, door, path

2. Turrets, roofs, windows

3. Flags, clouds

4. Tree trunks, trees, shrubs

instructions

Use ¼" (0.75 cm) seam allowance unless noted otherwise. Patterns are provided, beginning on page 127.

1. With right sides together and raw edges matching, sew sky to ground as shown (fig. 1-1). Press seam toward darker fabric.

2. Iron paper-backed fusible adhesive to wrong side of appliqué motif fabrics, following manufacturer's directions. Pin patterns to right side of fabrics and cut out shapes. Peel off paper backing (page 116).

3. Fuse flag foreground to flag background (fig. 1-2).

4. Position appliqués onto sky–ground background, as shown. Using iron, fuse in position. Fuse in order shown (fig. 1-3). Fuse flag above turret. Use zigzag or satin stitch for flagpole.

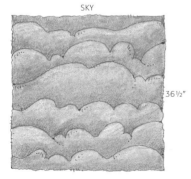

SKY

36½"

36½"

24½"

GROUND

fig. 1-1

fig. 1-2

fig. 1-3

5. Sew around exposed edges of appliqués with free-motion straight stitches (page 117). Outline background shapes first, working toward foreground (fig. 1-4). Free-motion stitching looks best if you sew over stitching lines at least three times. The repeated lines blend together visually, adding a nice hand-drawn look to the finished piece. If desired, stitch around appliqués with satin stitch or blanket stitch.

6. Using chalk, air-soluble ink, or other temporary marker, draw details on roofs and turrets. Add shingles and bricks (fig. 1-5). Stitch all details using free-motion sewing (page 117).

7. Stitch details on trees, bushes, clouds, and tree trunks (fig. 1-6).

8. Draw vines, then stitch; add leaves in groups of three or five (fig. 1-7).

9. For flowers, use variegated thread and stitch spiral circles. Add some satin stitch flower buds, taking advantage of programmed embroidery stitches on your sewing machine (fig. 1-8).

fig. 1-4

•tip•

Use a stabilizer under fabric for machine embroidery. When stitching is finished, slowly remove stabilizer, taking care to avoid ripping out any stitches.

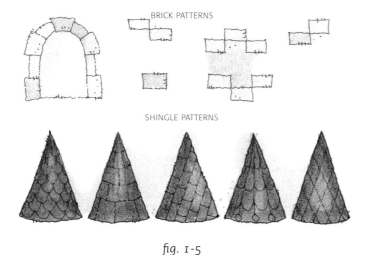

BRICK PATTERNS

SHINGLE PATTERNS

fig. 1-5

fig. 1-7

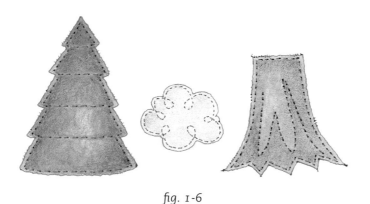

fig. 1-6

fig. 1-8

10. Square up quilt top with ruler and rotary cutter.

11. With right sides together and raw edges matching, pin 6½″ × 62″ (16.25 cm × 157.5 cm) inside borders to sides of quilt. Stitch in place, then press borders open. Repeat for top and bottom edges, this time using 6½″ × 52″ (16.25 cm × 132 cm) border strips (fig. 1-9).

12. Sew outside borders to all edges, as in Step 11 (fig. 1-10). Side border strips are 6½″ × 74″ (16.25 cm × 188 cm); top and bottom border strips are 6½″ × 64″ (16.25 cm × 162.5 cm).

13. For backing, sew 12″ (30 cm) strip to either side of larger backing piece (fig. 1-11).

14. Place backing fabric on table, right side down, then center batting on top. Center quilt top as top layer, right side up. Baste layers together with safety pins or thread, working from center toward edges (fig. 1-12).

fig. 1-9

fig. 1-10

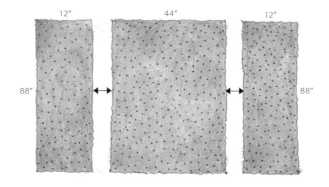

fig. 1-11

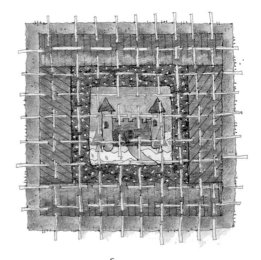

fig. 1-12

15. Quilt by hand or machine through all layers. For machine quilting, use free-motion technique (page 117). Outline castle, turrets, trees, and other elements (fig. 1-13a). Use stipple quilting for sky (fig. 1-13b). Where appropriate, use fabric design as quilting guideline (fig. 1-13c).

16. Square up quilt, using ruler and rotary cutter.

17. Fold under end of bias binding ½″ (1.25cm) and press. With right sides together and beginning with folded end, pin bias binding to front of quilt. Miter corners (page 120). Overlap bias ends. Stitch in place through all layers (fig. 1-14).

18. Trim away half the seam allowance. Fold binding over raw edges to back of quilt. Secure with invisible hand stitches (fig. 1-15).

fig. 1-13a

fig. 1-14

fig. 1-13b   fig. 1-13c

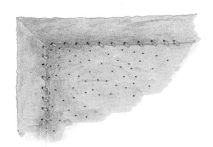

fig. 1-15

fig. 1-16

pillow sham

* *

Appliqué a castle in the clouds, then add a ruffle to complete this charming pillow sham. Finished size is 26″ × 32″ (65 cm × 80 cm)

instructions

Use ½″ (1.25 cm) seam allowance unless otherwise noted. Patterns are provided, beginning on page 127.

1. Prepare appliqués (page 115).

2. Position appliqués on pillow top. Using iron, fuse in position, working from background to foreground, in order shown (fig. 1-16). Fuse base cloud, then turrets, turret roofs, windows, and clouds.

Supplies

Fabric	Piece	Amount	Cut	Size
Pillow				
B	Pillow front	¾ yd (0.75 m)	1	22″ × 28″ (55 cm × 70 cm)
B	Pillow back	¾ yd (0.75 m)	2	17″ × 22″ (42.5 cm × 55 cm)
A	Ruffle	¾ yd (0.75 m)	6	4″ × 44″ (10 cm × 110 cm)
Motif				
C	Front right turret	12″ × 12″	1	3″ × 6″ (7.5 cm × 15 cm)
	Front left turret	(30 cm × 30 cm)	1	4″ × 8″ (10 cm × 20 cm)
	Center turret		1	5″ × 9″ (13 cm × 23 cm)
G	2 tall turrets	9″ × 10″ (22.5 cm × 25 cm)	2	2″ × 10″ (5 cm × 25 cm)
E	5 roofs	10″ × 12″ (25 cm × 30 cm)	See pattern	See pattern
F	Windows	6″ × 8″ (15 cm × 20 cm)	4 wide 3 narrow	See pattern
N	Base cloud, 3 upper clouds	½ yd (0.5 m)	1 each	See pattern
D	5 lower clouds	7″ × 20″ (17.5 cm × 50 cm)	See pattern	See pattern

3. Sew around exposed edges of appliqués with free-motion straight stitches (page 117). Outline background shapes first, working toward foreground (fig. 1-17).

4. Draw shingles with chalk or air-soluble pen (see fig. 1-5 for shingle patterns). Stitch by machine, using free-motion technique (page 118).

5. Using French seams (page 10), sew six ruffle sections together along short sides, making one long strip (fig. 1-18). Join ends to make a circle.

6. Hem along one long edge, using machine ¼"- (0.75 cm-) rolled-edge foot (fig. 1-19).

7. Mark quarter-points on ruffle; mark centerpoint on each side of pillow top.

8. Starting ¼" (0.75 cm) from top edge and using longest machine stitch length, sew two rows of gathering stitches along the top edge of ruffle; the rows should be ¼" (0.75 cm) apart (fig. 1-20). Sew a separate set of gathering threads in each section to avoid breaking threads.

•option•

Two gathering threads are recommended (Step 8), but if you want to make a perfect ruffle, use three gathering threads. When attaching the ruffle, sew along the middle thread. Remove the bottom gathering thread after the ruffle is attached.

fig. 1-17

fig. 1-18

fig. 1-19

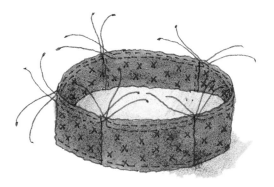

fig. 1-20

french seam

1. With wrong sides together, stitch a ¹⁄₁₆″ (0.25 cm) seam. Press.

2. Turn so right sides are together. Stitch a ¼″ (0.75 cm) seam, enclosing raw edges inside the seam.

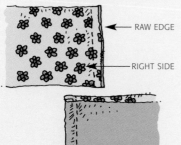

← RAW EDGE

← RIGHT SIDE

WRONG SIDE

9. Square up pillow top, using ruler and rotary cutter. With right sides together, pin ruffle to pillow top, matching marked points. Avoid placing ruffle seams at corners. Pull gathering threads to form ruffle.

10. Distribute gathers evenly, allowing extra fullness around corners. Pin. Stitch close to second row of gathering stitches (fig. 1-21). To stitch around corners, sew three stitches diagonally across corner point. When turned right side out, corner will look square and will lie flat (fig. 1-22).

11. Finish center edge of pillow backs by turning up raw edge ¼″ (0.75 cm), then ½″ (1.25 cm), forming a double-fold hem. Machine stitch along fold through all layers to hem (fig. 1-23).

12. Stack top and bottom pieces, right sides together, keeping ruffle inside and matching outside raw edges. Hemmed center back edges will overlap 3″ (7.5 cm). Using ⅝″ (1.75 cm) seam allowance, stitch around outside edges (fig. 1-24). Clip corners and turn right side out.

13. Insert pillow through opening in back of sham.

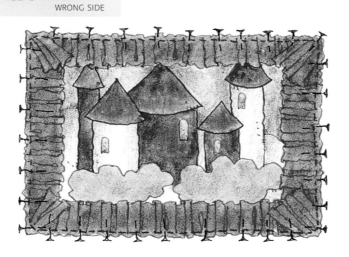

fig. 1-21

fig. 1-22

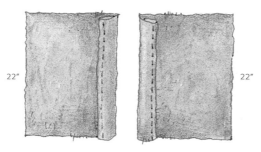

22″   22″

fig. 1-23

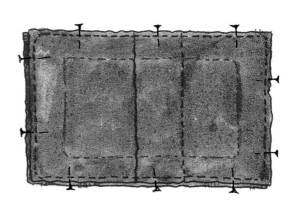

fig. 1-24

petal pillow

This charming flower pillow has softly stuffed petals. It can also be used to hold pajamas or nightgown for a little princess. Finished size is for 12″ (30 cm) round pillow.

Supplies

Fabric	Piece	Amount	Cut	Size
E	Pillow front	½ yd (0.5 m)	1 circle	13″ (32.5 cm) diameter
	Pillow backs		2	See pattern
C	Large petals	½ yd (0.5 m)	8	See pattern
D	Small petals	½ yd (0.5 m)	8	See pattern
	Flower center	scrap	1 circle	5″ (12.5 cm) diameter

instructions

Use ½″ (1.25 cm) seam allowance unless otherwise noted. Patterns are provided, beginning on page 127.

1. Pin front and back petals, right sides together. Sew, leaving small end open (fig. 1-25). Make four large petals and four small petals.

2. Lightly stuff all petals.

3. Position four large petals around center point of the pillow top. Make small gathers and pleats to keep the small ends close together. Stitch through all layers, securing open petal ends to pillow top (fig. 1-26).

•option•

Insert nightwear instead of pillow form. Add Velcro strips to the back sections, if desired, as an added closure.

fig. 1-25

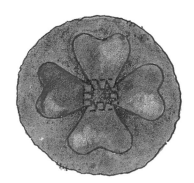

fig. 1-26

fig. 1-27

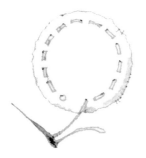

fig. 1-28

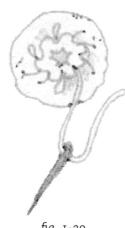

fig. 1-29

4. Add small petals as in Step 3, but position smaller petals over spaces between larger petals (fig. 1-27).

5. Make hand running stitches around edge of 5″ (12.5 cm) circle (fig. 1-28).

6. Pull threads gently; add small amount of stuffing. Pull thread again to close; lock stitches in place (fig. 1-29).

7. Position in center of flower, gathered edges down. Secure with ladder stitch (fig. 1-30).

8. Make pillow backs. Turn up straight edge ¼″ (0.75 cm), then ½″ (1.25 cm), forming a double-fold hem. Stitch along fold through all layers to hem (fig. 1-31).

9. Pin one pillow back on pillow front, right sides together. Lift up petals as needed. Join with machine stitches around outside edge (fig. 1-32).

10. Repeat Step 9 for remaining pillow back, overlapping back pieces 2″ (5 cm).

11. Turn pillow right side out (fig. 1-33). Insert 12″ (30 cm) round pillow form.

fig. 1-30

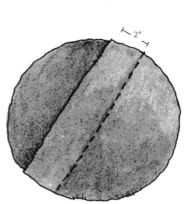

fig. 1-31

fig. 1-32

fig. 1-33

window valance

Three castle banners make a perfect window treatment for this princess bedroom. The center banner features an initial capped with a golden crown. Finished size of each banner is 12″ × 15″ (30 cm × 37.5 cm); three banners will fit a standard-sized window, 36″–37″ (90 cm–92.5 cm) wide. Rod pocket will accommodate rod up to 2½″ (6.25 cm) wide.

Supplies

Fabric	Piece	Amount	Cut	Size
Valance				
E	Front, dark	¼ yd (0.25 m)	2 each	See patterns
D	Front, light	½ yd (0.5 m)	See patterns	See pattern
O	Backing	¾ yd (0.75 m)	3	See pattern
	Rod pocket		3	4″ × 12″ (10 cm × 30 cm)
	Fusible batting	¾ yd (0.75 m)		
	Tassels, 3½″ (8.75 cm) purchased		3	
Motif				
D	Large heart	5″ × 10″ (12.5 cm × 25 cm)	2	See pattern
	Medium heart	5″ × 15″ (12.5 cm × 37.5 cm)	3	See pattern
E	Small heart	4″ × 4″ (10 cm × 10 cm)	1	See pattern
	Large star	5″ × 15″ (12.5 cm × 37.5 cm)	2	See pattern
	Small star	4″ × 12″ (10 cm × 30 cm)	1	See pattern
	Crown	4″ × 4″ (10 cm × 10 cm)	1	See pattern
	Initial	6″ × 9″ (15 cm × 22.5 cm)	1	See pattern

instructions

Use ½″ (1.25 cm) seam allowance unless otherwise noted. Patterns are provided, beginning on page 127.

1. Following drawings, join sections to make front of each of three banners (fig. 1-34)

2. Prepare heart, crown, and star appliqués (see page 115). Fuse two medium hearts on top of two large hearts; fuse one small heart on top of one medium heart (fig. 1-35).

3. Fuse hearts, stars, crown, and initial to banners, as shown (fig. 1-36). (For initial on center banner, see alphabet, page 127. Enlarge to measure 7½″ (19 cm) high.)

4. Stitch around outside edge of each motif with free-motion straight stitches (see page 117).

5. Trim ½″ (1.25 cm) off all sides of batting. Center fusible batting on wrong side of each back piece (fig. 1-37). Fuse in place, following manufacturer's directions.

6. Hem short ends of each rod pocket by turning up edges ¼″ (0.75 cm), then ½″ (1.25 cm), forming a double-fold hem. Stitch in place along fold through all layers. Turn up one long edge ⅜″ (1 cm). Press (fig. 1-38).

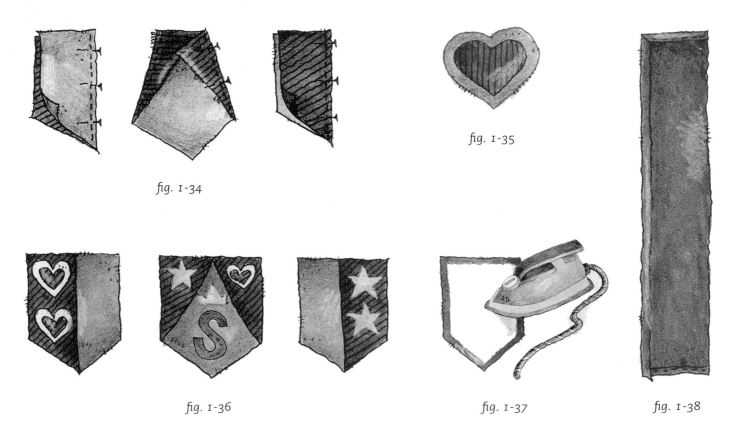

fig. 1-34

fig. 1-35

fig. 1-36

fig. 1-37

fig. 1-38

7. Pin a rod pocket on each back piece, right sides up, raw edges matching along top edge. Stitch through all layers along edge, inside seam allowance (fig. 1-39).

8. Pin valance front on valance back, right sides together. Using ½″ (1.25 cm) seam allowance, sew around all edges close to batting, leaving an 8″ (20 cm) opening on center top edge for turning (fig. 1-40).

9. Clip corners, trim edges, and turn right side out. Close opening with ladder stitch.

10. Using monofilament thread, quilt by machine along seamlines and edges of appliqués, taking care to keep rod pocket out of the way. Topstitch ½″ (1.25 cm) from edge along sides and bottom (fig. 1-41).

11. Sew bottom edge of rod pocket in place, using invisible hand stitches (fig. 1-42).

12. Sew tassel to bottom point of each banner (fig. 1-43).

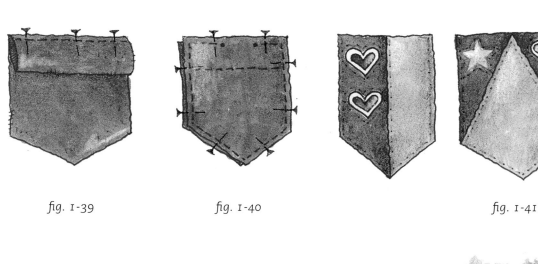

fig. 1-39   fig. 1-40   fig. 1-41

fig. 1-42

fig. 1-43

For detailed information on making perfect ruffles, see page 122.

•tip•

For detailed information on making perfect ruffles, see page 122.

dust ruffle

Complete the bed ensemble with a simple gathered dust ruffle. The ruffle is attached to three sides only. It is open at each bottom corner to allow for bedposts. Finished size is for twin bed, 39″ × 75″ (97.5 cm × 187.5 cm).

Supplies

Fabric	Piece	Amount	Cut	Size
Muslin	Deck	2¼ yd (2.1 m)	1	40″ × 76½″ (100 cm × 191.25 cm)
B	Ruffle	4 yd (3.7 m)	8	Each, 16″ × 44″ (40 cm × 110 cm)
			2	Each, 16″ × 22″ (40 cm × 55 cm)

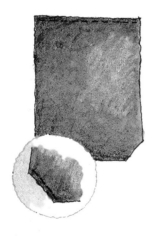

fig. 1-44

instructions

Use ½″ (1.25 cm) seam allowance unless otherwise noted.

1. Hem one short end of deck piece by turning up ¼″ (0.75 cm), then ½″ (1.25 cm) forming a double-fold hem. Hem bottom two corners of deck by turning up diagonal fold ¼″ (0.75 cm), then ½″ (1.25 cm), again forming a double-fold hem. Press and stitch in place (fig. 1-44).

2. Make end ruffle by joining two 16″ × 44″ (40 cm × 110 cm) pieces. Make two side ruffles by joining three 16″ × 44″ (40 cm × 110 cm) pieces plus one 16″ × 22″ (40 cm × 55 cm) piece (fig. 1-45).

fig. 1-45

3. Hem two short ends on each ruffle by folding up ¼″ (0.75 cm), then ½″ (1.25 cm), to form a double-fold hem. Using a machine ¼″- (0.75 cm-) rolled-edge foot, hem the bottom edge of each ruffle (fig. 1-46).

4. Starting ¼″ (0.75 cm) from top edge, and using the longest machine stitch length setting, sew two rows of gathering stitches along the top edge of each ruffle; rows should be ¼″ (0.75 cm) apart. Gather each section separately (fig. 1-47).

5. Mark quarter-points on each ruffle and each side of deck.

6. With right sides together, pin end ruffle to end of deck, matching quarter-points. Pull threads to gather ruffle. Pin carefully, then stitch in place between gathering threads (fig. 1-48). Add side ruffles in same manner.

7. Topstitch ruffles to deck from back, stitching next to seamline. The extra line of stitching adds strength to the seam and helps the ruffle hang better (fig. 1-49).

lampshade

Cover a lampshade with fabric, using craft glue to hold. Cover raw edges with decorative braid; add a ruffle along the bottom edge. Or, look for a lampshade with a self-adhesive cover. Simply remove the paper wrapper and press your fabric onto the shade.

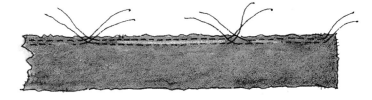

fig. 1-46

fig. 1-47

fig. 1-48

fig. 1-49

princess bed swag

A swag above the princess's bed adds a royal look to this enchanted bedroom. This easy bit of elegance can be made in about an hour. Finished length is 160" (4 m).

Supplies

Fabric	Piece	Amount	Cut	Size
A	Swag	2⅓ yd (2.2 m)	1	84" × 44" (210 cm × 110 cm)
B	Swag lining	2⅓ yd (2.2 m)	2	84" × 22" (210 cm × 55 cm)
	Hardware for hanging swag			See figs. 1-55a-b

instructions

Use ½" (1.25 cm) seam allowance unless noted otherwise.

1. Trim selvages, then cut swag yardage in half lengthwise (fig. 1-50).

2. With right sides together, join by stitching at one short end. Press seam open (fig. 1-51).

3. Repeat Steps 1 and 2 for lining.

4. Trim swag ends to make corner angle (fig. 1-52). Repeat for lining.

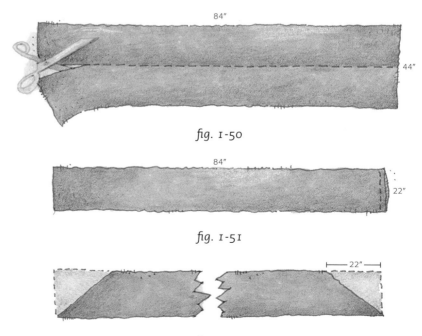

fig. 1-50

fig. 1-51

fig. 1-52

5. With right sides together and matching raw edges, pin lining to swag. Stitch around outside edge, leaving a 12″ (30 cm) opening along the center of one long side (fig. 1-53).

6. Clip corners; turn right side out. Press carefully. Use invisible stitches to close opening.

7. Using accordion pleats about every 3½″ (8.75 cm), fold swag. Lining will show at each end (fig. 1-54). Finger-press swag and use pins or masking tape to hold folds in place. If you wait a few days before removing pins and hanging the swag, the soft folds will drape better.

8. Hang swag over bed, following mounting diagram (fig. 1-55a). Swag will also look wonderful as a window treatment (fig. 1-55b).

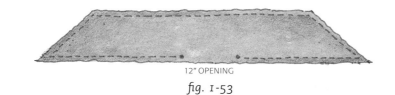

12″ OPENING

fig. 1-53

fig. 1-54

fig. 1-55a

fig. 1-55b

tiny tooth fairy bag

Put toddler's baby tooth in this Lilliputian-sized felt bag, then place it where the Tooth Fairy can find it easily in a darkened bedroom. Hang it on a doorknob, dangle it from a drawer pull, or pin it to a dresser lampshade. Finished size is 2″ × 3″ (5 cm × 7.5 cm).

Supplies

Fabric	Piece	Amount	Cut	Size
A (felt)	Pouch		1	5¾″ × 2″ (14.5 cm × 5 cm)
B (felt)	Body	2″ × 2″ (5 cm × 5 cm)	1	See pattern
C (felt)	Apron	2″ × 2″ (5 cm × 5 cm)	1	See pattern
D (felt)	Wings	3″ × 1″ (7.5 cm × 2.5 cm)	1	See pattern
Embroidery floss		1	6″ (15 cm) strand	
Ribbon, ⅛″ (0.5 cm) wide		1	8″ (20 cm) long	
Embroidery needle				
White glue				
¾″ (2 cm) covered button and muslin	Face	1	1	See package
Doll hair	Hair	Scraps or yarn		

instructions

Patterns are provided, beginning on page 127.

1. Glue wings to one end of pouch; glue body to other end. Glue apron on top of body (fig. 1-56).

2. Fold ends toward middle and pin in place so wings overlap body. Sew sides together, using embroidery floss and buttonhole stitch (fig. 1-57).

3. Using an embroidery needle large enough to accommodate ⅛″ (0.5 cm) ribbon, thread ribbon for handle. Make a knot in one end. Pull through top fold and knot again to hold in place. Leave 8″ (20 cm) length for handle, then knot ribbon on other side in same manner (fig. 1-58). Use a dab of white glue or fray-checking liquid to secure knots.

4. For face, cover a button with flesh-colored muslin, following manufacturer's directions. Draw features with permanent fine-point marker. Add blush on cheeks and chin. Glue hair in place (fig. 1-59).

5. Sew face button in place. For collar, glue a bit of lace under face button. Use another dab of glue to keep face button from turning (fig. 1-60).

•option•

This Tiny Tooth Fairy Bag is appropriate for a little boy, too. Make it in his favorite colors or use colors that match his room decor. Glue hair on top of head only.

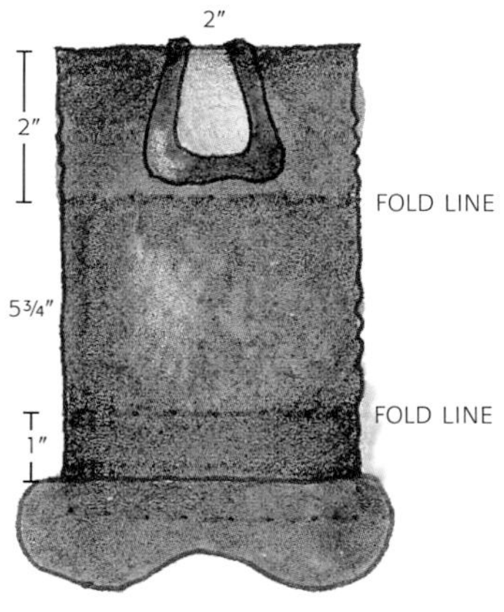

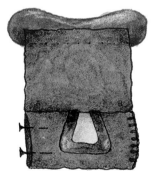

2″

2″

FOLD LINE

5¾″

T 1″

FOLD LINE

fig. 1-56

fig. 1-57

fig. 1-58

fig. 1-59

fig. 1-60

Trucks and Treasures
Little Boy's Bedroom

Young construction workers will dream of wondrous things to build in this irresistible bedroom. The bedspread features Courthouse Steps blocks, built around a truck motif fabric. Look for trucks on the pillow sham, along the dust ruffle, and at the window. Accessories include traffic sign pillows and a teddy bear holding a laundry bag.

fabric recommendations

Cotton

Cotton/polyester blends

Decorator fabrics

Projects shown use fourteen coordinating fabrics.

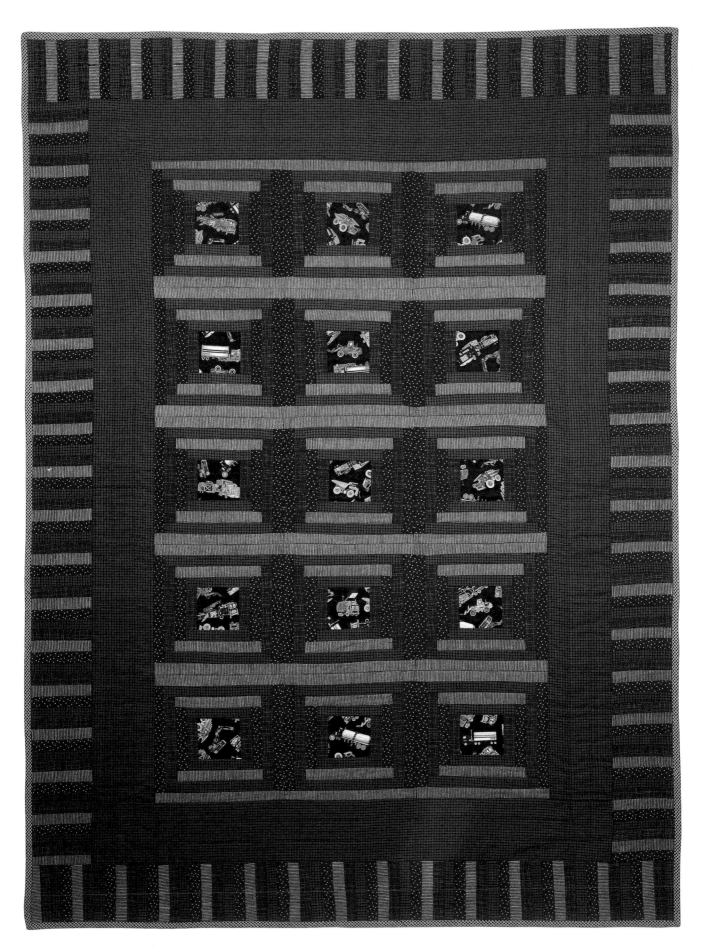

courthouse steps quilt

••

This quilt features easy-to-piece Courthouse Steps blocks. The center squares use motifs from printed fabric. Finished size is for twin bed, 60" × 84" (152.4 cm × 213.4 cm).

Supplies

Fabric	Piece	Amount	Cut	Size
A	Center of block	1 yd (1 m)	15 squares	Each 4½" × 4½" (11.25 cm × 11.25 cm)
B	Part of block	⅓ yd (0.3 m)	7 strips	Each 1½" × 44" (3.75 cm × 110 cm)
C	Part of block	½ yd (0.5 m)	11 strips	Each 1½" × 44" (3.75 cm × 110 cm)
D	Part of block	½ yd (0.5 m)	11 strips	Each 1½" × 44" (3.75 cm × 110 cm)
E	Part of block	⅝ yd (0.65 m)	15 strips	Each 1½" × 44" (3.75 cm × 110 cm)
Solid border (sample uses C)	Inside border	1¾ yd (1.6 m)	2 strips	Each 6½" × 62" (16.25 cm × 157 cm)
			2 strips	Each 6½" × 51" (16.25 cm × 127 cm)
Pieced border (sample uses B, C, D, and E)	Outside border	⅝ yd (0.65 m) each	48 strips (see Step 9)	Each 1½" × 44" (3.75 cm × 110 cm) (sample uses 12 of each color)
A	Backing	5 yd (4.5 m)	1	44" × 90" (110 cm × 228 cm)
			2	12" × 90" (30 cm × 228 cm)
	Batting	Twin size		
N	Extra-wide double-fold bias tape	8½ yd (7.6 m)		

How to cut motifs from patterned fabric

- Cut an 8" × 8" (20 cm × 20 cm) piece of cardboard or template plastic.

- Cut an opening in the center, 4½" × 4½" (11.25 cm × 11.25 cm). This is the template.

- Use template to identify usable design motifs (fig 2-1).

- Center motifs in template opening.

- Trace around template opening; cut out motif.

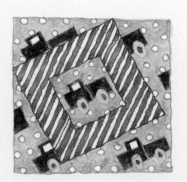

fig. 2-1

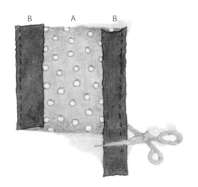

fig. 2-2

instructions

Use ¼″ (0.75 cm) seams throughout unless otherwise noted.

1. Sew strip B to right and left sides of center square. Trim off excess strip length (fig. 2-2). Press seams toward darker fabric.

2. Sew strip C to top and bottom edges. Trim away excess and press as in Step 1 (fig. 2-3).

3. Sew strip D to right and left sides of block. Trim away excess and press (fig. 2-4).

4. Sew strip E to top and bottom edges. Trim and press (fig. 2-5).

5. Repeat Steps 1–4 to complete block (fig. 2-6). Make 15 blocks, each 12½″ (31.25 cm) square. Square up blocks, using ruler and rotary cutter.

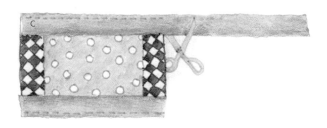

fig. 2-3

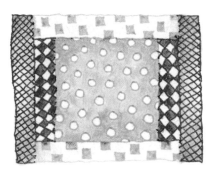

fig. 2-4

fig. 2-5

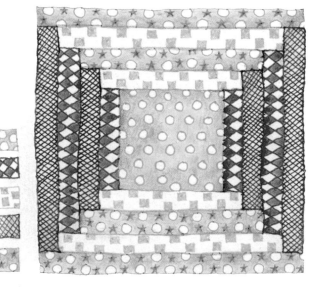

fig. 2-6

6. Sew blocks together along sides to make five rows of three blocks (fig. 2-7). Join rows at top and bottom (fig. 2-8).

7. Square up quilt top, using ruler and rotary cutter.

8. Sew 6½" × 62" (16.25 cm × 155 cm) border to sides of quilt (fig. 2-9). Trim excess length; press. Sew 6½" × 51" (16.25 cm × 127 cm) border to top and bottom of quilt (fig. 2-10). Trim excess length; press.

9. To piece outer border, arrange 1½" (3.75 cm) strips in a pleasing order. (Sample shown alternates red and blue strips.) Sew 12 strips together to make a strip set; press (fig. 2-11). Make a total of four strip sets.

10. Cut across strip set at 6½" (16.25 cm) intervals (fig. 2-12).

11. Join six pieces at the ends to make border for one side; repeat. Join five pieces at the ends to make border for top; repeat for bottom edge.

•tip•

Measure quilt before cutting border strips (Step 9). Be sure your strips are a little longer than needed. Most cotton fabrics are 44" (110 cm) wide, so that width determines how long each strip is. If your fabric is slightly wider or narrower, just cut 1½" (3.75 cm) strips across the width of the fabric and they will be fine. If your fabric is especially narrow, cut a few extra strips.

fig. 2-7

fig. 2-9

fig. 2-10

fig. 2-8

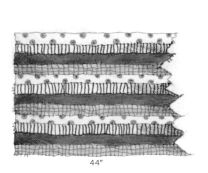

44"

fig. 2-11

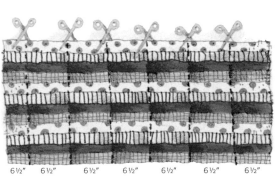

6½" 6½" 6½" 6½" 6½" 6½" 6½"

fig. 2-12

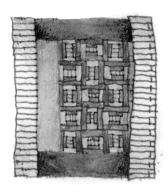

fig. 2-13

fig. 2-14

12. Pin border strips to right and left edges, right sides together, then sew through all layers. Trim away excess length, flip open, and press (fig. 2-13). Add borders to top and bottom edges in same way. Square up quilt top, using ruler and rotary cutter.

13. To make backing, pin a 12″ (30 cm) section to each side of the 44″-wide (110 cm-wide) section, right sides together. Stitch, flip open, and press (fig. 2-14).

14. Assemble layers and baste together.

15. Quilt by machine, stitching in the ditch along seamlines. For inner border, stitch two lines, each 2″ (5 cm) from edges. For outer border, stitch in the ditch along every third seamline (fig. 2-15). Square up quilt, using ruler and rotary cutter.

16. Fold under end of bias ½″ (1.25 cm) and press. With right sides together and beginning with folded end, pin bias binding strip to front side of quilt, matching raw edges. Miter corners (fig. 2-16 and page 120). Overlap bias ends. Stitch in place through all layers.

17. Trim away half the seam allowance. Fold bias to back of quilt, covering raw edges. Sew to back of quilt with invisible hand stitches (fig. 2-17).

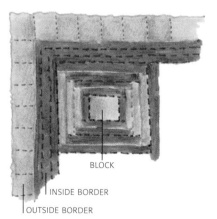

BLOCK

INSIDE BORDER

OUTSIDE BORDER

fig. 2-15

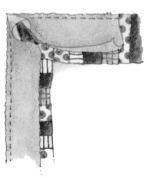

fig. 2-16

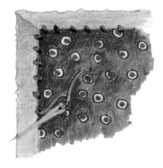

fig. 2-17

pillow sham

Appliqué this truck to the top of a pillow sham so your young driver will be headed down the road for a good night's sleep. Finished size is 27″ × 33″ (67.5 cm × 82.5 cm).

Supplies

Fabric	Piece	Amount	Cut	Size
F	Pillow sham front	1⅝ yd (1.5 m)*	1	28″ × 34″ (70 cm × 85 cm)
F	Pillow sham back		2	18½″ × 28″ (46 cm × 70 cm)
Motif				
G	Tractor (cab)	5″ × 6″ (12.5 cm × 15 cm)	1	See pattern
H	Window	Scrap	1	2″ × 2″ (5 cm × 5 cm)
D	Trailer	Scrap	1	7″ × 18″ (17.5 cm × 45 cm)
I	Wheels	Scrap	5	3″ (7.5 cm) circle
J	Hubs	Scrap	5	1½″ (3.75 cm) circle
B	Fenders	3½″ (8.75 cm) circle	5	See pattern
G	Wide stripe	4″ × 11″ (10 cm × 28 cm)	1	See pattern
E	Narrow stripe	3″ × 11″ (7.5 cm × 28 cm)	1	See pattern
E	Smokestack	Scrap	1	½″ × 9″ (1.25 cm × 23 cm)
J	Smoke	6″ × 6″ (15 cm × 15 cm)	2	See pattern

*Allow extra if using directional fabric.

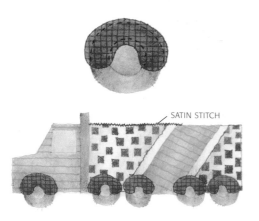

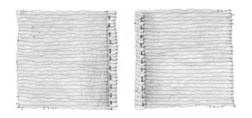

SATIN STITCH

fig. 2-18

instructions

Use ½″ (1.25 cm) seams throughout unless otherwise noted. Patterns provided, beginning on page 127.

1. Using paper-backed fusible adhesive, prepare appliqués (page 115) for fenders, hubcaps, wheels, trailer, smokestack, smoke, cab, cab window. For stripes, cut first fabric (narrow stripe), then fuse on top of second fabric (wide stripe). Fuse onto trailer as one stripe.

2. Position appliqués as shown (fig. 2-18). Fuse in position. Stitch around all edges with machine satin stitch.

3. Finish center edge of pillow backs by turning up raw edge ¼″ (0.75 cm), then ½″ (1.25 cm), forming a double-fold hem. Machine stitch along fold through all layers to hem (fig. 2-19).

4. Stack top and bottom pieces, right sides together, matching outside raw edges. Hemmed center back edges will overlap approximately 3″ (7.5 cm). Stitch around outside edges (fig. 2-20). Clip corners and turn right side out.

5. To make flange, stitch by machine on right side, 3″ (7.5 cm) from finished edge (fig. 2-21).

6. Insert pillow through opening in back of sham.

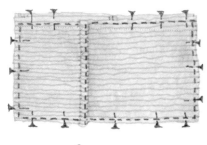

fig. 2-19

fig. 2-20

fig. 2-21

3″

traffic sign pillows

Make these traffic sign pillows to decorate a young driver's bed. During playtime, they can mark important spots along imaginary roads that run under the bed and along the playroom wall. Finished size is 12" to 15" (30 cm to 37.5 cm).

Supplies

Fabric	Piece	Amount	Cut	Size
Speed Limit				
L	Background	½ yd (0.5 m)	2	13" × 16" (32.5 cm × 40 cm)
I	Letters	3" × 25" (7.5 cm × 62.5 cm)		See pattern
Stop				
K	Background	½ yd (0.5 m)	2	See pattern
L	Letters	4" × 12" (10 cm × 30 cm)		See pattern
Yield				
H	Background	½ yd (0.5 cm)	2	See pattern
I	Letters	3" × 13" (7.5 cm × 32.5 cm)		See pattern
Polyester fiber stuffing				

instructions

Use ½" (1.25 cm) seams throughout unless otherwise noted. Patterns are provided, beginning on page 127.

Each pillow is constructed as follows:

1. Cut out background fabric, following pattern for Stop and Yield signs. Round off corners for Speed Limit sign (fig. 2-22).

2. Prepare appliqués (page 115). Enlarge as desired ("STOP" and "50" are 3½" (9 cm) high; other letters are 2¼" (5.7 cm) high).

3. Position and center letters and numbers on background fabric as shown, then fuse in place.

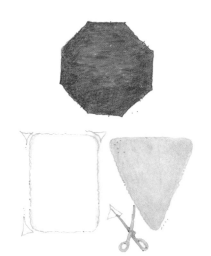

fig. 2-22

For a whimsical touch, make up your own signs; for example, "Jason Sleeps Here," "Quiet Zone," "Night Night," or "Dream Land." If you want a sign with longer words, turn the rectangular pillow sideways or make the pillow larger.

dust ruffle

Appliqué a convoy of trucks motoring around the bed. Purchase a solid-color dust ruffle with box pleats, not gathers. Appliqué truck motifs, as for Pillow Sham, page 115. Use leftover scraps from the quilt, but vary them within each truck. Two motifs will fit on each side of the bed skirt and one will fit across the foot.

4. Using machine satin stitch, stitch around all edges of letters and numbers. Add a satin stitched line near outside edge, as shown (fig. 2-23). Here are two ways to make a raised satin stitch line: stitch a narrow 2 mm line, then stitch a 3 mm line on top of the first one; or, using your machine's cording foot, satin stitch over thin cord, such as gimp.

5. With right sides together, pin pillow front to pillow back. Trim back to match front (front may be smaller due to appliqué satin stitches). Stitch around outside edges, leaving a 4″ (10 cm) opening for turning. Be sure that the opening for turning is along a straight edge between corners (fig. 2-24). For extra strength, stitch a second line immediately next to the first one.

6. Clip curves and corners; turn right side out. Press seam from right side. Stuff pillow medium-firm until it holds the desired shape. To stuff pillow, leave an opening large enough for your hand to go through. Start stuffing in corners and edges, working toward middle and bottom opening. Use large handfuls of stuffing; too-small clumps will make your pillow lumpy. Close opening with ladder stitch (page 119).

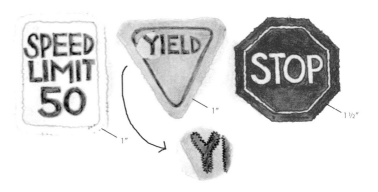

fig. 2-23

fig. 2-24

window valance

•••

Little boys will enjoy pretending that this truck is parked at the window. Customize by adding child's name to the license plate. Finished size is 42" × 21" (105 cm × 52.5 cm). This valence will fit a standard-sized window, 36"–37" (90 cm–92.5 cm) wide.

Supplies

Fabric	Piece	Amount	Cut	Size
Valance				
K	Valance front (body)	½ yd (0.5 m)	1	44" × 16" (110 cm × 40 cm)
White muslin	Valance lining	⅝ yd (0.6 m)	1	44" × 16" (110 cm × 40 cm)
	Rod pocket		1	4½" × 42" (11.25 cm × 105 cm)
Fusible batting	Valance batting	½ yd (0.5 m)	1	42" × 14" (105 cm × 35 cm)
	Tire batting		2	5½" × 6½" (13.75 cm × 16.25 cm)
Curtain rod				2½" (6.25 cm) wide × window width
Motif				
K	Body	See above	1	44" × 16" (110 cm × 40 cm)
J	Bumper	¼ yd (0.25 m)	1	6" × 44" (15 cm × 110 cm)
H	Headlights	Scrap	2	Each 5" (12.5 cm) circle
H	Turn signal (yellow)	Scrap	2	Each 5" × 4" (12.5 cm × 10 cm)
M	Turn signal (red)	Scrap	2	Each 4" × 3" (10 cm × 7.5 cm)
F	Grille	Scrap	1	16" × 6" (40 cm × 15 cm)
I	Tires	¼ yd (0.25 m)	4	Each 6" × 7" (15 cm × 17.5 cm)
I	Letters	Scrap		See pattern
G	License	Scrap	1	8" × 4" (20 cm × 10 cm)

instructions

Use ½″ (1.25 cm) seams throughout unless otherwise noted. Patterns provided, beginning on page 127.

1. Fuse bumper fabric to paper-backed fusible adhesive. Fold 6″ × 44″ (15 cm × 110 cm) strip in half and cut as shown (fig. 2-25).

2. Prepare appliqués (page 115) for license plate and letters. Curve corners on license plate. Fuse letters onto license. Center license on bumper; fuse (fig. 2-26).

3. Prepare appliqués for headlights, turn signals, and grille. Curve all corners on rectangles. Pin appliqués on right side of truck body, as shown (fig. 2-27). Fuse in position. Stitch around appliqué edges with machine satin stitch.

4. Curve bottom corners on tires. Center fusible fleece to wrong side of tire front. Fuse in position, taking care not to flatten batting.

5. Pin tire front to tire back, right sides together. Sew along three sides (fig. 2-28). Clip corners and turn right side out.

6. For tread lines, sew three lines through all layers. Use a decorative stitch for tire tread (fig. 2-29). Repeat Steps 4–6 for second tire.

7. Using ½″ (1.25 cm) seam allowance, sew tires to bottom of valance as shown in placement diagram (fig. 2-27).

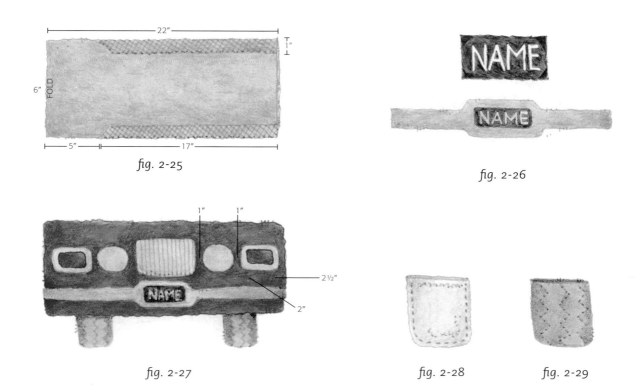

fig. 2-25

fig. 2-26

fig. 2-27

fig. 2-28

fig. 2-29

8. For rod pocket, turn up short ends ¼″ (0.75 cm), then ½″ (1.25 cm), forming a double-fold hem. Stitch through all layers. Turn up bottom edge ¼″ (1.25 cm) and press.

9. With right sides up, center rod pocket along top edge of valance backing. Stitch inside seam allowance (fig. 2-30).

10. Center batting on wrong side of valance backing, leaving approximately ¾″ (0.75 cm) all around. Fuse in place.

11. Pin valance front to valance back, right sides together, folding tires to inside. Using ½″ (1.25 cm) seam allowance, sew around all edges, leaving an 8″ (20 cm) opening on center bottom edge for turning (fig. 2-31).

12. Clip corners, trim edges, and turn right side out. Close opening with invisible stitches.

13. Topstitch ¼″ (0.75 cm) from edges, except around tires.

14. Quilt valance with monofilament thread along edges of appliqués, about ¼″ (0.75 cm) away from satin stitches. Stitch vertical lines through grille. Quilt a long horizontal line through middle of bumper; stitch in the ditch around license plate (fig. 2-32).

15. Secure bottom edge of rod pocket to valance back with invisible hand stitches (fig. 2-33).

•option•

This valance is shown hanging from a regular curtain rod, but it could also be tacked onto a cornice or mounted on the wall for a headboard.

fig. 2-30

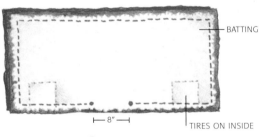

fig. 2-31

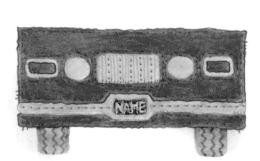

fig. 2-32

fig. 2-33

teddy bear laundry bag

This hanging bear welcomes dirty clothes with open arms. A wire armature inside the bear gives added support. Finished size is 27" × 34" (67.5 cm × 85 cm).

Supplies

Fabric	Piece	Amount	Cut	Size
B	Bear arms, head	¾ yd (0.75 m)	2 each	See patterns
	Ears		4	See pattern
C	Paw pads	Scrap	2	See pattern
I	Nose	Scrap	1	See pattern
I	Eyes	Scrap	2	1" (2.5 cm) diameter circle
A	Laundry bag	⅞ yd (0.9 m)	2	22" × 26" (55 cm × 65 cm)
¼" (0.75 cm) satin ribbon			¼ yd (0.25 m)	6" (15 cm) long
⅝" (1.75 m) satin ribbon			1⅓ yd (1.3 m)	46" (115 cm) long
Heavy wire coat hanger				

instructions

Use ½" (1.25 cm) seams throughout unless otherwise noted. Patterns are provided, beginning on page 127.

1. Using paper-backed fusible adhesive, prepare paw appliqués (see page 115). Position paws on arms as shown on pattern, then fuse in place. Sew around each paw with machine satin stitch (fig. 2-34).

fig. 2-34

2. Prepare eye and nose appliqués. Position on front head fabric, then fuse in place. Using machine satin stitch, embroider bear's face: stitch a line from nose to mouth, stitch mouth, stitch around nose and eyes (fig. 2-35).

3. Pin one ear on top of another, right sides together. Using ¼″ (0.75 cm) seam allowance, stitch around edge, leaving bottom of ear open (fig. 2-36). Clip curves and turn right side out. Repeat for second ear.

4. Stuff lightly. Make small ½″ (1.25 cm) pleat on bottom edge of ears. Stitch ears closed, using ⅛″ (0.5 cm) seam allowance (fig. 2-37).

5. Pin ears to bear face as shown. Sew in place, stitching in seam allowance. Pin ribbon hanger to top edge of bear's face. Machine stitch in position in seam allowance (fig. 2-38).

6. With right sides together, sew bear face to front arms. Repeat for bear back head and back arm pieces (fig. 2-39).

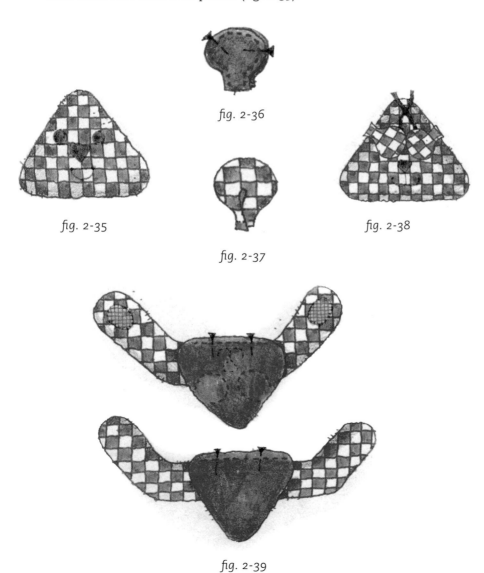

fig. 2-36

fig. 2-35

fig. 2-37

fig. 2-38

fig. 2-39

•option•

Embroider facial details with hand stitches. Or, use fabric pens with nontoxic permanent ink to outline features. Avoid using beads and other removable trims that a toddler could pull off and swallow.

7. Pin bear front to bear back. Sew around edges. Square off corners where bear head meets bear shoulder, leaving a 7″ (17.5 cm) opening in bottom edge (fig. 2-40). Backstitch over ears and ribbon to reinforce seam.

8. Clip curves and into corners (fig. 2-41). Turn right side out. Stuff head firmly.

9. Make armature for arms by untwisting coat hanger and bending into desired shape. Hook ends together, then pinch closed.

10. Stuff neck and paws, then insert armature into arms. Stuff arms, taking care to keep armature in place with stuffing all around it. Close opening with ladder stitch (page 119).

11. For laundry bag, cut two laundry bag pieces as shown in diagram (fig. 2-42).

12. For each side opening on laundry bag, make a narrow double-fold hem by turning up raw edge ⅛″ (0.5 cm), then ¼″ (0.75 cm). Machine stitch through all layers to hem (fig. 2-43).

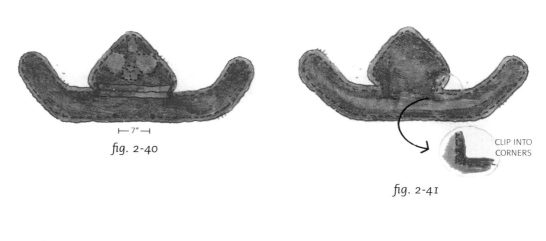

7″

fig. 2-40

CLIP INTO CORNERS

fig. 2-41

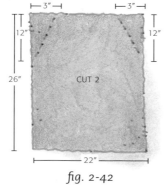

3″
3″
12″
12″
26″
CUT 2
22″

fig. 2-42

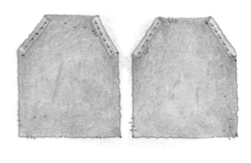

fig. 2-43

13. With right sides together and using ¼″ (0.75 cm) seam allowance, sew bag front to bag back, stitching around sides and bottom (fig. 2-44). For extra strength, stitch a second seam immediately next to the first. Turn right side out.

14. To finish neck edge, gather up each top edge to 7″ (17.5 cm), as shown (fig. 2-45).

15. Place edges on ribbon as shown, then pin along bottom edge of ribbon, wrong sides together (fig. 2-46). Stitch.

16. Fold ribbon over raw edge, trimming excess fabric as needed. Topstitch along both neck edges, stopping at each tie (fig. 2-47).

17. Hang laundry bag on bear's arms. Tie ribbon (fig. 2-48).

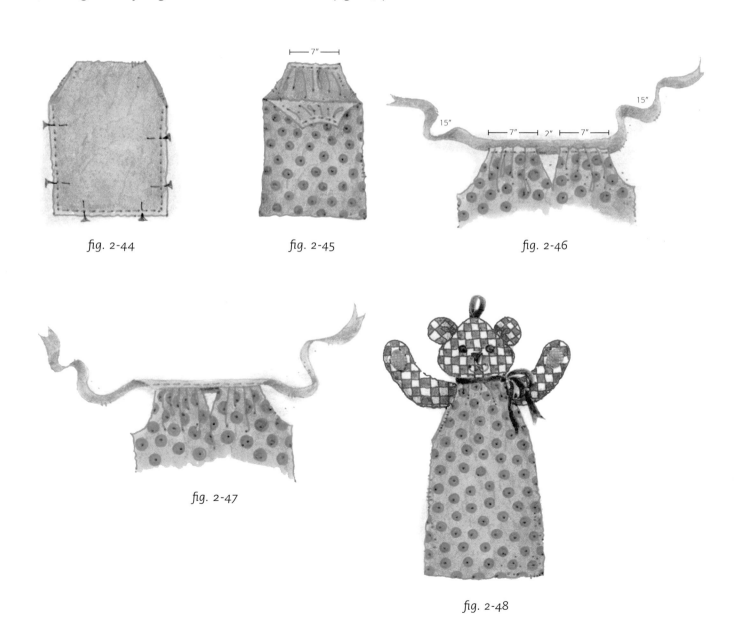

fig. 2-44

fig. 2-45

fig. 2-46

fig. 2-47

fig. 2-48

Apple for the Teacher
Nursery School Necessities

3

Children love to go to nursery school. These bright and cheerful items will make them feel like big kids. Make an art smock with your child's name on the front. The coordinating lunch sack, backpack, and naptime mat are quick and easy to make, too. For extra practice with numbers, use this colorful felt counting board. It can be rolled up and taken anywhere.

fabric recommendations

Cotton

Cotton/polyester blend

Vinyl-coated fabric

Felt

Projects shown use three coordinating fabrics.

naptime mat

Make a special mat for naptime at nursery school. For easy storage, mat can be rolled up and tied. The mat is pieced and quilted in one step, using a flip-and-sew technique. Finished size is 27" × 42" (67.5 cm × 105 cm).

Supplies

Fabric	Piece	Amount	Cut	Size
A	Backing	1 yd (1 m)	1	44" × 29" (110 cm × 72.5 cm)
A	Top	¾ yd (0.75 m)	3	27" × 6½" (67.5 cm × 16.25 cm)
B	Top	½ yd (0.5 m)	2	27" × 6½" (67.5 cm × 16.25 cm)
C	Top	½ yd (0.5 m)	2	27" × 6½" (67.5 cm × 16.25 cm)
	Batting	1 yd (1 m)	1	44" × 29" (110 cm × 72.5 cm)
A	Extra-wide double-fold bias tape	4¼ yd (4 m)		
½" (1.25 cm) grosgrain ribbon		1 yd (1 m)		
A or B	Matching pillow (optional)	½ yd (0.5 m)	1	13¼" × 40½" (33 cm × 101.25 cm)

instructions

Use ¼" (0.75 cm) seam allowance unless otherwise noted.

fig. 3-1

1. Place backing on table, wrong side up. Place batting on top. Pin top A at one end, right side up. Pin B on top of A, right sides together. Stitch along inside edge through all layers. Flip B open and press (fig. 3-1).

2. Pin top C on top B, right sides together. Stitch along inside edge through all layers. Flip C open and press.

3. Continue adding top pieces until top is completed (fig. 3-2).

4. Center ribbon on back of mat along one short edge. Stitch in seam allowance through all layers (fig. 3-3).

5. Fold under end of bias ½″ (1.25 cm) and press. With right sides together, begin with folded end: pin bias binding strip to back of mat, matching raw edges and covering ribbon tie (fig. 3-4). Miter corners (see page 120). Overlap bias ends. Stitch in place, backstitching over ribbon to reinforce.

6. Trim away half the seam allowance. Fold binding to front of quilt, covering raw edges. Topstitch in place along folded edge (fig. 3-5).

7. To store mat, fold in thirds lengthwise, then roll toward end with ribbon. Wrap ribbons around roll and tie (fig. 3-6).

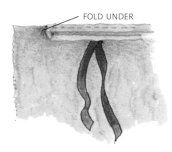

fig. 3-4

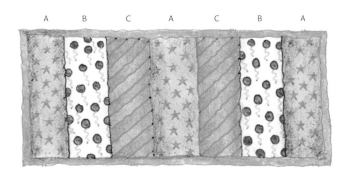

fig. 3-2

fig. 3-3

fig. 3-5

fig. 3-6

naptime pillow

Cut one piece of fabric, 13¼″ × 40½″ (33 cm × 101.25 cm).

Fold up short ends ¼″ (0.75 cm), then ¾″ (2 cm). Stitch through all layers to form a double-fold hem. Fold one end 9″ (22.5 cm) toward middle, right sides together (fig. 3-7). Fold over other end so that ends overlap and pillow is 17″ (42.5 cm) long. Stitch sides closed, using ½″ (1.25 cm) seam allowance.

Turn right side out. Insert 12″ × 16″ (30 cm × 40 cm) pillow.

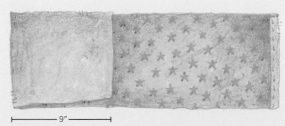

|←——— 9″ ———→|

fig. 3-7

number banner

Use this felt banner to help little ones learn to count. Felt pieces are fun for Mother to cut and easy for little fingers to handle. Finished size is 28″ × 36″ (70 cm × 90 cm).

Supplies

Fabric	Piece	Amount	Cut	Size
Felt	Background	1 yd (1 m)	1	28″ × 38″ (70 cm × 95 cm)
Felt	Letters	3 rectangles	See patterns	9″ × 12″ (22.5 cm × 30 cm)
Felt	Numbers	3 rectangles	See patterns	9″ × 12″ (22.5 cm × 30 cm)
Felt	Various shapes	9″ × 12″ (22.5 cm × 30 cm) rectangles	See patterns	9″ × 12″ (22.5 cm × 30 cm)
⅛″ (0.5 cm) ribbon	Border lines	8½ yd (8 m)		

White craft glue

Fabric paint, markers

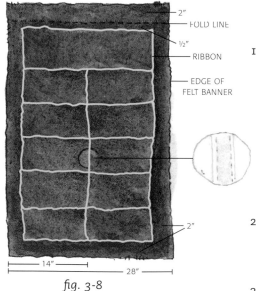

fig. 3-8

instructions

Patterns provided, beginning on page 127.

1. Sew ribbon onto background as shown. Use twin needle and catch both edges of narrow ribbon at the same time. Because ¹⁄₁₆″ (0.25 cm) ribbon is too narrow to miter at corners, sew to corner point and stop with needle in the down position. Turn over (twist) ribbon twice, lift presser foot, then reposition at 90° angle. Pivot fabric with twin needle in the down position and continue sewing. Apply ribbon with ribbon foot or glue ribbon in place. Sew center vertical strip first, then horizontal rows, then outside border (fig. 3-8).

2. Prepare appliqués (page 115). Enlarge letters and numbers to be 2¼″ (5.7 cm) high. Position letters and numbers, then fuse in place as in photo.

3. Use freezer paper for shapes: trace shapes onto paper side, then iron waxy side onto back of felt. Press freezer paper lightly to felt so it will be easy to remove. Cut out shapes.

4. Glue details on flower, balls, butterflies, fish, and rabbits. Use fabric paint or fabric marker to draw eye on fish and faces on rabbits (fig. 3-9).

5. Fold top 2″ (5 cm) of banner toward back, forming a rod pocket. Stitch through all layers using monofilament thread (fig. 3-10).

6. Arrange shapes on board. If desired, use Velcro to hold shapes in place.

fig. 3-9

BACK BANNER

fig. 3-10

art smock

Every young artist needs a smock to protect school clothes. This smock is open in the back to make it easy to put on. The pocket on the front holds crayons and other special tools.

instructions

Use ½" (1.25 cm) seam allowance unless otherwise noted. Patterns are provided, beginning on page 127.

1. Fold pattern crosswise, then lengthwise. Place pattern along two fold lines. Cut out smock and lining pieces. Unfold and cut through center back to make back openings.

Supplies

Fabric	Piece	Amount	Cut	Size
Smock				
B	Smock	½ yd (0.5 m)	1	See pattern
A	Smock lining	½ yd (0.5 m)	1	See pattern
C	Pocket	Scrap	1	4½" × 11" (11.25 cm × 28 cm)
A	Pocket lining	Scrap	1	4½" × 11" (11.25 cm × 28 cm)
	⅞" (2.25 cm) Ribbon ties	1¾ yd (1.6 m)		
¾" (2 cm) Velcro	2" (5 cm)			
Palette motif				
	Palette	5" × 5" (12.5 cm × 12.5 cm)		See pattern
	Letters	3" × 3" (7.5 cm × 7.5 cm) each		See pattern
	Letter blocks	3" × 3" (7.5 cm × 7.5 cm) each		1 per letter
	Paint blobs	2" × 2" (5 cm × 5 cm) each	3	See pattern
	Brush handles	3" × 6" (7.5 cm × 15 cm) each	2	See pattern
	"Metal" brush tips	2" × 2" (5 cm × 5 cm) each	2	See pattern
	Brushes	2" × 2" (5 cm × 5 cm) each	2	See pattern

2. With right sides together, pin pocket to pocket lining. Stitch around outside edge, leaving a 3″–4″ (7.5–10 cm) opening for turning (fig. 3-11). Clip corners, turn right side out, and press.

3. Position pocket on smock front as on pattern. Topstitch along side and bottom edges. Stitch through pocket from top to bottom at center, then divide one section in half again (fig. 3-12).

4. Prepare appliqués (see page 115), enlarging letters as desired. Make a pleasing arrangement on smock front. Fuse, then stitch around all edges.

5. Cut ribbon into 4 equal lengths. Pin ties in place on wrong side of smock front and backs. Stitch in seam allowance (fig. 3-13).

6. For neckline closure, stitch Velcro squares on right side of smock back and smock lining (fig. 3-14).

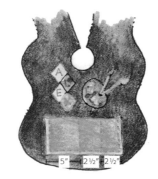

fig. 3-12

7. With right sides together, pin smock lining to smock, taking care to keep ties inside. Stitch around outside edges, backstitching over ribbons to reinforce and leaving a 6″ (15 cm) opening for turning (fig. 3-15).

8. Turn smock right side out; press. Topstitch along outside edges (fig. 3-16), closing the opening used for turning.

fig. 3-13

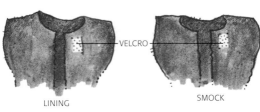

fig. 3-14

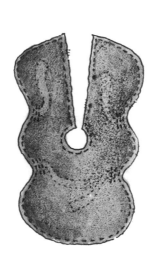

fig. 3-15

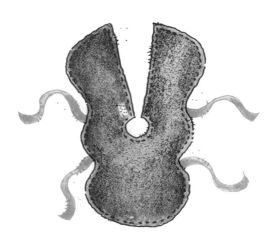

fig. 3-16

backpack

· ·

Send your toddler to nursery school with show-and-tell items safely stored in this adorable backpack. Fusible vinyl makes colorful cotton fabrics moisture- and stain-resistant. Finished size is 8" wide × 9" long × 4" deep (20 cm wide × 22.5 cm long × 10 cm deep).

Supplies

Fabric	Piece	Amount	Cut	Size
C	Backpack	½ yd (0.5 m)	2	11" × 14" (238 cm × 35 cm)
B	Lining	½ yd (0.5 m)	2	11" × 14" (238 cm × 35 cm)
	Backpack straps	½ yd (0.5 m)	1	3" × 44" (7.5 cm × 110 cm)
	D-ring straps		1	3" × 6" (7.5 cm × 15 cm)
A	Flap		1	8" × 10" (20 cm × 25 cm)
C	Flap lining		1	8" × 10" (20 cm × 25 cm)
Fusible vinyl	Backpack flap	½ yd (0.5 m)	2	10½" × 13½" (26 cm × 33.7 cm)
			1	7½" × 8½" (18.75 cm × 21.5 cm)
Heavyweight fusible interfacing	Backpack	¾ yd (0.75 m)	2	10½" × 13½" (26 cm × 33.75 cm)
	Backpack straps		1	2½" × 44" (6.25 cm × 110 cm)
	D-ring straps		1	2½" × 6" (6.25 cm × 15 cm)
1" (2.5 cm) D-rings		4		
Jeans or topstitching needle (100/16)				
¼" (0.75 cm) drawstring cord		1 yd (1 m)		
Extra-wide double-fold bias tape		1 yd (1 m)		
¾" (2 cm) Velcro	Flap closure	2" (5 cm)		

instructions

Use ½″ (1.25 cm) seam allowance unless otherwise noted.

1. Fuse iron-on vinyl to right side of backpack fabric. Fuse iron-on interfacing to wrong side of backpack fabric.

2. Make ¾″ (2 cm) machine buttonhole on backpack front, centered ½″ (1.25 cm) from top edge (fig. 3-17).

3. Right sides together, stack lining pieces. Stitch along three sides (fig. 3-18).

4. To make box corner on lining, fold corner so that side and bottom seams match. This will make a point at end of bottom seam. Stitch 4½″ (11.25 cm) seam across end as shown; trim off point (fig. 3-19).

5. Fuse iron-on vinyl to right side of flap fabric. Fuse iron-on interfacing to wrong side of flap fabric. Curve two corners as shown (fig. 3-20).

6. Center fuzzy Velcro strip on right side of flap lining, 1″ (2.5 cm) from straight edge. Stitch in place (fig. 3-21).

7. Right sides together, pin flap lining to flap. Stitch around outside flap edges, leaving opening for turning (fig. 3-22). Trim lining to match flap.

•tip•

Always use a pressing cloth or vinyl backing paper when ironing vinyl-coated fabric.

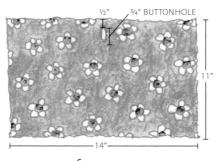

fig. 3-17

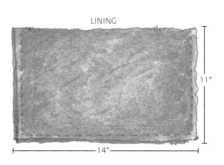

fig. 3-18

fig. 3-19

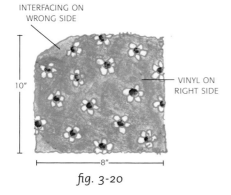

fig. 3-20

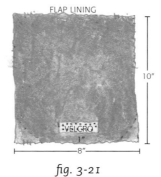

fig. 3-21

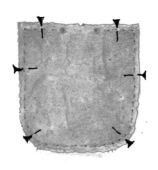

fig. 3-22

8. Clip curves and corners; turn flap right side out; press.

9. Fuse interfacing to 6″ (15 cm) strap. Fold over one long edge ¾″ (2 cm); double-fold the other edge ⅜″ (1 cm), then ⅝″ (1.75 cm). Strap will be approximately 1″ (2.5 cm) wide (fig. 3-23). Press.

10. On wrong side of strap, zigzag along centerfold through all layers. Top-stitch along each outside edge. Cut in half to make two 3″ (7.5 cm) lengths (fig. 3-24).

11. Slip one end through two D-rings. Repeat for remaining 3″ (7.5 cm) strap (fig. 3-25).

12. Fuse interfacing to 44″ (110 cm) strap. Fold strap as in Step 9. Press.

13. Make a folded point at end: fold over end ¼″ (0.75 cm), then fold edges at 45° angle toward middle, centering point in 1″-wide (2.5 cm-wide) section (fig. 3-26). Note that folds are off-center.

14. Zigzag through all layers as in Step 10. Topstitch edges. Cut in half to make two 22″ (55 cm) straps (fig. 3-27).

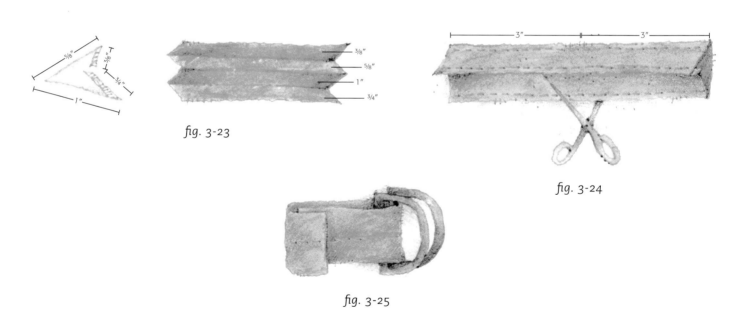

fig. 3-23

fig. 3-24

fig. 3-25

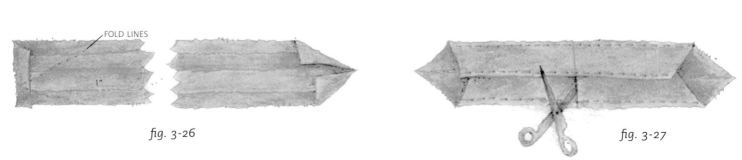

fig. 3-26

fig. 3-27

15. Sew both 22″ (55 cm) straps to lining side of flap (fig. 3-28).

16. With right sides together, position flap on backpack. Topstitch through all layers, closing flap opening. Attach D-rings (fig. 3-29).

17. With right sides together, stack backpack pieces, keeping flap and straps inside. Stitch along three sides as shown (fig. 3-30).

18. Make box corners as in Step 4, stitching 5″ (12.5 cm) seam across bottom point. Turn right side out.

19. Insert lining in backpack, wrong sides together, matching side seams and top edges. Pin bias tape over top edge. Stitch in place from front, overlapping and folding under top end for a neat finish (fig. 3-31).

20. For casing, stitch through all layers, 1″ (2.5 cm) from top edge, *keeping buttonhole within casing*. Be careful not to catch flap in seam. Thread ¼″ (0.75 cm) cord through casing. Knot both ends of cord (fig. 3-32).

21. Mark position of flap closure, then sew hook Velcro to front of backpack, stitching through all layers.

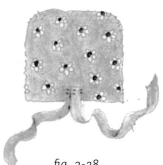

fig. 3-28

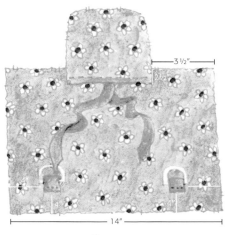

fig. 3-29

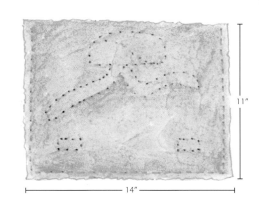

fig. 3-30

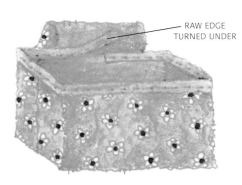

RAW EDGE TURNED UNDER

fig. 3-31

fig. 3-32

rain poncho

· ·

Rainy days will be fun days when your toddler has a bright poncho and rain hat to wear. Fusible vinyl makes bright cotton prints water-resistant.

Supplies

Fabric	Piece	Amount	Cut	Size
C	Poncho	1⅜ yd (1.3 m)	4	18″ × 23″ (45 cm × 57.5 cm) See pattern
A	Placket	¼ yd (0.25 m)	2	3½″ × 20″ (8.75 cm × 50 cm)
A	Extra-wide double-fold bias tape	¾ yd (0.75 m)		
17″ (42.5 cm) wide fusible vinyl		3 yds (2.75 m)	4	17″ × 22″ (42.5 cm × 55 cm)
			2	3″ × 19″ (7.5 cm × 47.5 cm)
¾″ (2 cm) buttons		3		

•tip•

Fuse vinyl to fabric before cutting out pattern pieces.

instructions

Use ½″ (1.25 cm) seam allowance unless noted otherwise.

1. Fuse iron-on vinyl to right side of each 18″ × 23″ (45 cm × 57.5 cm) poncho section. *Always* use a pressing cloth when ironing vinyl coated fabric. Pin poncho fabrics together, right sides facing. This ensures that you'll have right front and left front pieces, and right back and left back pieces. Using pattern, cut two fronts and two backs (fig. 3-33).

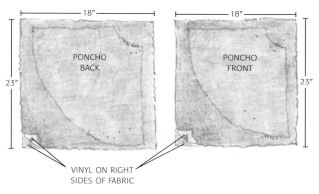

fig. 3-33

2. Fuse vinyl to right side of placket fabric. Fold up one 20″ (50 cm) edge of placket ⅜″ (1 cm); press using pressing cloth (fig. 3-34).

3. Pin unfolded, right side of placket on wrong side of poncho front, matching edges. Stitch as shown (fig. 3-35). With front of poncho up, press placket toward outside edge.

4. Fold placket toward front of poncho 1½″ (3.75 cm); seam will be inside placket (fig. 3-36). Press; topstitch along folded edge (fig. 3-37).

5. Repeat Steps 3–5 for remaining poncho front.

6. Pin backs together, right sides facing. Stitch along center back (fig. 3-38).

7. Open seam allowance; press. Topstitch with twin needle, straddling seam.

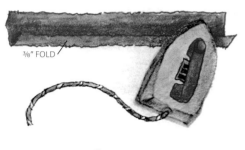

fig. 3-34

fig. 3-35

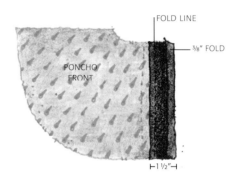

fig. 3-36

fig. 3-37

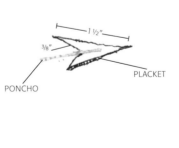

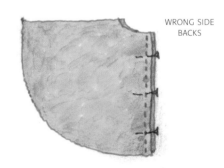

fig. 3-38

8. Join fronts to back at shoulders (fig. 3-39). Open seam allowance on shoulder seams; press. Topstitch with twin needle (fig. 3-40).

9. With right side of bias against wrong side of poncho, pin bias along neck, folding in ends at neck edge. Stitch from back in seam allowance (fig. 3-41).

10. Fold bias to neck front, covering raw edges and enclosing seamline. Topstitch from front (fig. 3-42).

11. Turn up bottom edge ⅜″ (1 cm) to form hem. Stitch from front with twin needle.

12. Starting 1″ (2.5 cm) from neckline, mark placement for three ⅞″ (2.25 cm) buttonholes, each 3½″ (8.75 cm) apart. Stitch buttonholes by machine. Mark button placement; sew on buttons (fig. 3-43).

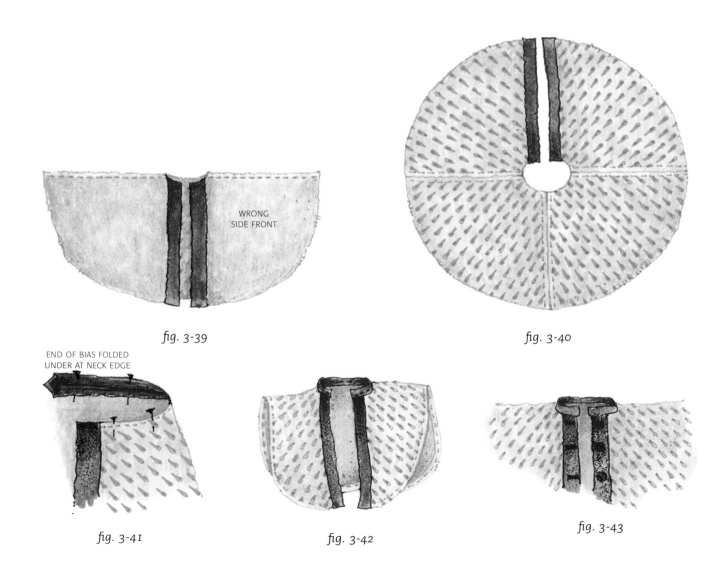

fig. 3-39

fig. 3-40

fig. 3-41

fig. 3-42

fig. 3-43

rain hat

Protect your child's head from rain showers with this charming rain hat. Add an umbrella and boots for jumping and splashing in puddles.

Supplies

Fabric	Piece	Amount	Cut	Size
Fusible vinyl		1½ yd (1.4 m)	1	6½″ × 29½″ (16.25 cm × 73.75 cm)
			2	15½″ × 15½″ (38.75 cm × 38.75 cm)
B	Crown	½ yd (0.5 m)	6	7″ × 30″ (17.5 cm × 75 cm)
C	Crown lining	½ yd (0.5 m)	6	See pattern
C	Brim	16″ × 16″ (40 cm × 40 cm)	2	See pattern
C	Brim lining	16″ × 16″ (40 cm × 40 cm)	2	See pattern

instructions

Use ¼″ (0.75 cm) seam allowance unless noted otherwise. Patterns are provided, beginning on page 127.

1. Fuse iron-on vinyl to right side of crown and brim fabric. Always use a pressing cloth when ironing vinyl-coated fabric. Cut out pattern pieces.

2. To make front crown, pin one crown piece on top of another, right sides together. Sew from large end toward point, stopping ¼″ (0.75 cm) from point (fig. 3-44). Open and press. Repeat, adding a crown piece to other side of first piece. This is now the front crown (fig. 3-45). Clip curves as needed.

3. Make back crown the same as front, following Step 2.

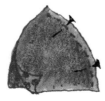

fig. 3-44

fig. 3-45

4. Pin front crown to back crown, right sides together. Sew across top of crown as shown (fig. 3-46). Open and clip curves as needed.

5. Repeat Steps 2–4 to make crown lining.

6. Pin brim ends with right sides together. Stitch across ends (fig. 3-47); open into a circle; press. Repeat for brim lining.

7. With right sides together and matching center back seams, pin brim to brim lining along outside edge. Stitch around outside edge (fig. 3-48).

8. Turn brim right side out; press. Topstitch ½″ (1.25 cm) from outside edge (fig. 3-49).

9. Pin crown lining inside crown, wrong sides together, matching seams. Pin brim to crown, right sides together. Stitch brim to crown, using ½″ (1.25 cm) seam (fig. 3-50). Trim seam to ¼″ (0.75 cm).

10. With seam allowance toward crown, topstitch in place from outside (fig. 3-51). Trim away excess seam allowance.

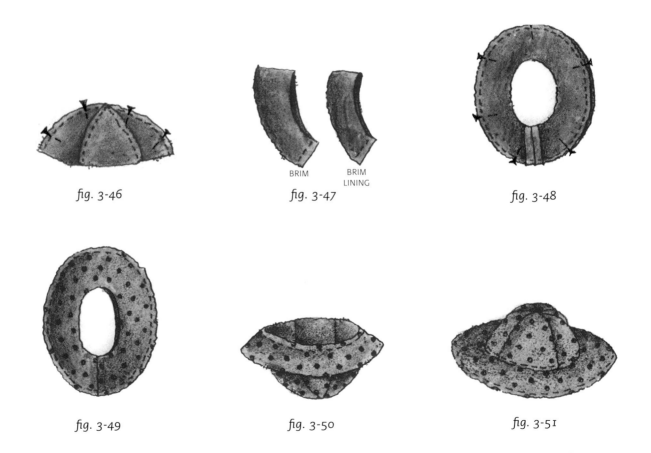

fig. 3-46

BRIM   BRIM LINING

fig. 3-47

fig. 3-48

fig. 3-49

fig. 3-50

fig. 3-51

snack sack

This easy-to-make sack is handy for carrying snack-time treats to school. The fleece lining adds thermal qualities; fusible vinyl makes it moisture-resistant and easy to clean. Finished size is 5″ × 6″ (12.5 cm × 15 cm).

Supplies

Fabric	Piece	Amount	Cut	Size
B	Sack	¼ yd (0.25 m)	2	8″ × 8½″ (20 cm × 21.25 cm)
C	Lining	¼ yd (0.25 cm)	2	8″ × 8½″ (20 cm × 21.25 cm)
	Flap		1	4″ × 9″ (10 cm × 22.5 cm)
	Batting	¼ yd (0.25 cm)	2	7½″ × 8″ (18.75 cm × 20 cm)
Heavyweight fusible interfacing		¼ yd (0.25 cm)		
C	Binding		1	2″ × 20″ (5 cm × 50 cm)
¾″ (1 cm) Velcro		2″ (5 cm)		
17″ (42.5 cm) wide fusible vinyl		¼ yd (0.25 cm)	4	7½″ × 8″ (18.75 cm × 20 cm)

instructions

Use ¼″ (0.75 cm) seam allowance unless otherwise noted.

1. Fuse iron-on vinyl to right side of sack and lining fabrics. Cut out pieces.

2. With right sides together, pin one sack piece on the other. Sew around sides and bottom edges (fig. 3-52).

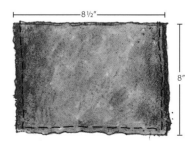

fig. 3-52

3. To make box corner, fold corner so that side and bottom seams match. This will make a point at end of bottom seam. Sew 3″ (7.5 cm) seam across ends, as shown; trim off point (fig. 3-53). Turn sack right side out.

4. Pin fleece to wrong side of vinyl-covered lining fabric. Make three quilting lines by stitching from top to bottom through all layers (fig. 3-54).

5. Using ¾″ (1 cm) seam allowance, assemble lining as in Step 2.

6. Make box corners as in Step 3, except sew 2½″ (6.25 cm) seam across point.

7. Pin lining inside sack, matching side seams and top edges. Pin to hold.

8. Pin binding strip over top edge. Stitch in place from front, using machine zigzag stitch, overlapping and folding under ends for a neat finish (fig. 3-55).

9. Fuse iron-on interfacing to wrong side of flap.

fig. 3-53

fig. 3-54

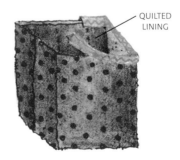

fig. 3-55

10. Center fuzzy Velcro strip on right side of flap, 1″ (2.5 cm) from foldline. Stitch in place (fig. 3-56).

11. Fold flap in half, right sides together. Stitch around outside edges, leaving an opening for turning (fig. 3-57).

12. Clip corners, turn flap right side out; press. Sew flap to back of sack, 1″ (2.5 cm) from top edge. Stitch through all layers, closing opening used for turning (fig. 3-58).

13. Mark position of flap closure, then sew hook Velcro to front, stitching through all layers (fig. 3-59).

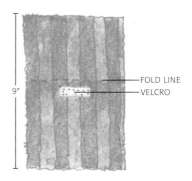

fig. 3-56

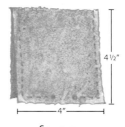

fig. 3-57

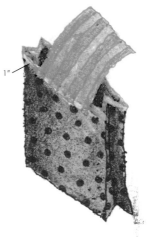

fig. 3-58

fig. 3-59

Portable Playroom

4

Toys and More for Imaginative Play

Encourage imaginative play by making these wonderful playroom items. Finger Puppets and an easy-to-store Tabletop Puppet Theater will inspire many hours of creative play. Make a special Tea-Time Set for your child to entertain dollies and other friends. Here's a table, cushioned tuffet, and all the linens for a perfect tea party.

fabric recommendations

Cotton

Cotton/polyester blend

Decorator fabric

Projects shown use seven coordinating fabrics.

tabletop puppet theater

This simple tabletop theater is a handy size for special performances. It's easy for Mother to store, too. Start with foam-core poster board, cover with fabric, add curtains, and the show can begin. Finished size is 18" × 24" (45 cm × 60 cm).

Supplies

Fabric/Materials	Piece	Amount	Cut	Size
¼" (0.75 cm) Foam-core board	1 Front	24" × 36" (60 cm × 90 cm)	1	18" × 24" (45 cm × 60 cm)
	4 Stands		2	3" × 8" (7.5 cm × 20 cm)
			2	2" × 3" (5 cm × 7.5 cm)
	8 Rod brackets		4	2" × 2" (5 cm × 5 cm)
			4	2" × ¾" (5 cm × 2 cm)
¼" (0.75 cm) dowel rod		20" (50 cm) long		
A	Frame covering	½ yd (0.5 m)	1	18" × 24" (45 cm × 60 cm)
C	Side curtains	¼ yd (0.5 m)	2	7" × 16½" (17.5 cm × 41.25 cm)
B	Top curtain (valance)	¼ yd (0.25 m)	1	5½" × 28" (13.75 cm × 70 cm)
Extra-wide double-fold bias tape	4 yds (3.7 m)			
½" (1.25 cm) decorative braid	4 yds (3.7 m)			
Tassel/fringe braid		½ yd (0.5 m)		
¼" (0.75 cm) cord		1½ yd (1.4 m)		
Acrylic paint				
X-acto knife, #11 blade				
White glue				

instructions

Make Theater Frame

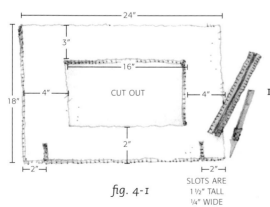

fig. 4-1

SLOTS ARE 1 ½" TALL ¼" WIDE

1. Using ruler and X-acto knife with #11 blade, cut 13" × 16" (32.5 cm × 40 cm) opening in foam-core board as shown. Cut two slots (fig. 4-1) on bottom edge.

2. Glue fabric to front, using white fabric glue. Let dry overnight, then cut out center opening, trimming fabric close to inside edges of foam-core board (fig. 4-2).

3. Cover all edges with bias tape and glue in place (fig. 4-3). Let glue dry.

4. Glue decorative braid or ribbon along front edges. For outside edges, start and end at slots on bottom. For inside edges, glue braid along sides and bottom edge only (fig. 4-4). To minimize raveling of braid ends, mark the length of braid required. On both sides of the braid, apply a generous amount of fray-checking liquid at the mark, about 1″ (2.5 cm) wide. Allow to dry. Cut in middle of sealed area (fig. 4-5).

5. Glue tassel braid across top inside edge. Glue bias tape over outer edge (fig. 4-6).

6. To make stand, curve top edges and cut slots as shown (fig. 4-7). Paint with acrylic paint to match fabric. Glue braid on top edges (fig. 4-8). Assemble as shown (fig. 4-9).

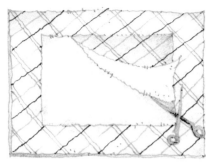

fig. 4-2

fig. 4-3

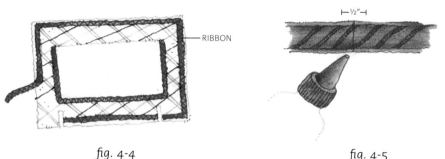

RIBBON

⊢½″⊣

fig. 4-4

fig. 4-5

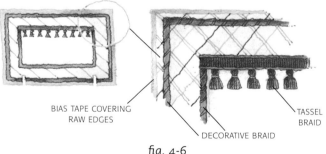

BIAS TAPE COVERING RAW EDGES

DECORATIVE BRAID

TASSEL BRAID

fig. 4-6

SLOT
1½″ DEEP
¼″ WIDE

8″

3″

1″ TALL
¼″ WIDE

fig. 4-7

SLOT
1″ DEEP
¼″ WIDE

2″

3″

fig. 4-8

fig. 4-9

Make Curtains

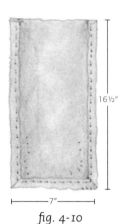

fig. 4-10

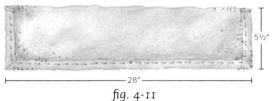

fig. 4-11

7. For side curtains, turn up side edges ¼″ (0.75 cm), then ¼″ (0.75 cm), forming a double-fold hem. Hem bottom edge in same way, by turning up ¼″ (0.75 cm), then ½″ (1.25 cm). Stitch through all layers, mitering corners (fig. 4-10).

8. For top valance, turn up side edges ¼″ (0.75 cm), then ½″ (1.25 cm), forming a double-fold hem. Hem bottom edge in same way. Stitch through all layers, mitering corners (fig. 4-11).

9. Make rod casing for curtains and valance by turning up top edge ¼″ (0.75 m), then ¾″ (2 cm), forming a double-fold hem. Stitch through all layers along fold line (fig. 4-12).

10. To make brackets for dowel rod, sandwich two small foam-core pieces between two large pieces as shown (fig. 4-13). Glue in place. Repeat for second bracket.

11. Glue rod brackets on back of theater, 1½″ (3.75 cm) from each corner, as shown (fig. 4-14). Let glue dry.

12. Thread curtains onto dowel rod, with valance in between side curtains. Insert dowel rod into brackets on back of theater (fig. 4-15).

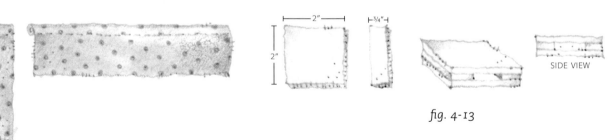

fig. 4-12

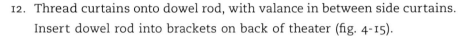

fig. 4-13

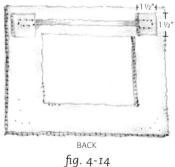

BACK

fig. 4-14

OPENING

BACK

fig. 4-15

finger puppets

These felt Finger Puppets are super-easy to make. Add a face and a few snippets of trim to make the characters spring to life. The puppets shown include Witch, Fairy Godmother, Puppy, Kitty, Dragon, Unicorn, and, of course, Prince and Princess.

Supplies Use an assortment of felt colors to make several puppets. Size given is for one puppet.

Fabric	Piece	Amount	Cut	Size
Felt	Puppet body	10" × 12" (25 cm × 30 cm)	2	1½" × 2½" (3.75 cm × 6.25 cm)
Felt in assorted colors	Costumes	Scraps		
Assorted trims				
Embroidery floss				
Fine-tip fabric marker				
White craft glue				

general instructions

1. Pin two body pieces together. Round off one end (fig. 4-16).

2. Glue on any felt pieces, such as spots, that will end up in the outside seam (see Puppy, for example).

3. Using three strands of embroidery floss, stitch around three sides with buttonhole stitch (fig. 4-17).

4. Draw face, using fine-tip fabric markers.

5. Add extra trims, such as dress, hat, laces, and ribbons.

fig. 4-16

fig. 4-17

fig. 4-18

fig. 4-19

specific instructions

6. *Hair:* Wind yarn around your fingers seven or eight times. Tie in middle; snip ends. Fluff to make a pompom (fig. 4-18). Baste to top of puppet's head. To make a "strip" of hair, wrap yarn around a bent coat hanger and sew down the middle, then cut loops (fig. 4-19).

7. *Ears:* Cut out ear shape; stitch in position. Kitty ears stand up; Puppy ears hang down.

8. *Snout:* A small oval shape glued at nose makes a good snout for Unicorn and Dragon.

9. *Dress and Coat:* Cut a dress shape and glue it to front of puppet. Two small rectangles will make a collar. Coat wraps around puppet (fig. 4-20).

10. *Hat:* For the crown, cut a quarter circle as shown; overlap edges, and glue or stitch. For the brim, cut a circle, then cut a 1″ (2.5 cm) circle out of the middle (fig. 4-21). Stitch crown to brim (fig. 4-22). Tack hat to puppet's head with a few basting stitches.

11. *Faces:* Simple faces are fine—copy the faces shown, or draw your own (fig. 4-23). Your child will supply the personality.

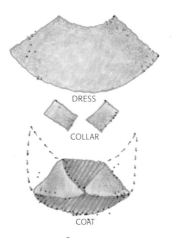

DRESS

COLLAR

COAT

fig. 4-20

2 1/4″

2 1/4″

CROWN

CUT OUT 1″

2 1/2″

fig. 4-21

fig. 4-22

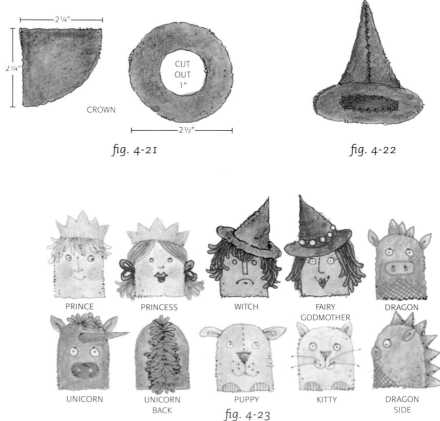

PRINCE PRINCESS WITCH FAIRY GODMOTHER DRAGON

UNICORN UNICORN BACK PUPPY KITTY DRAGON SIDE

fig. 4-23

tea-time table, table skirt, tablecloth, and linens

Shorten the legs on an inexpensive occasional table, then cover it with a skirt and tasseled tablecloth. Set the table with tiny place mats and napkins—and perhaps special tea party dishes.

Supplies

Fabric	Piece	Amount	Cut	Size
Purchased table: 19½″ (48.75 cm) diameter, 26″ (65 cm) high				
D	Top	¾ yd (0.75 m)	1	20″ (50 cm) circle
B	Skirt	1¾ yd (1.6 m)	3	20″ × 40″ (50 cm × 100 cm)
A	Tablecloth	1 yd (1 m)	1	34″ × 34″ (85 cm × 85 cm)
C, E	Placemat (1)		2	Each, 5½″ × 8½″ (13.75 cm × 21.25 cm)
G	Napkin (1)		1	10″ × 10″ (25 cm × 25 cm)
2½″ (6.25 cm) tassels			4	
Fusible batting			1	5″ × 8″ (12.5 cm × 20 cm)

instructions

Tea-Time Table

1. Project shown uses 19½″ (48.75 cm) round occasional table with screw-on legs. Cut off bottoms of legs so that when assembled, table will be 18″ (45 cm) high.

Table Skirt

Use ½″ (1.25 cm) seam allowance unless otherwise noted.

2. Join ends of skirt sections to make circle. Press seams open (fig. 4-24).

fig. 4-24

how to make pattern for any tabletop (either round or rectangular)

Place table upside-down on wrong side of fabric. Trace around tabletop, then cut out fabric, adding an additional ½″ (1.25 cm) all around for seam allowance (fig. 4-25).

fig. 4-25

For the table skirt, measure height of table. Measure circumference of table. Prepare a strip of fabric with a length equal to 2–2½ times the circumference and a width equal to the table height plus 2″ (5 cm).

3. Make a double-fold hem by turning up one edge ¼″ (0.75 cm), then 1″ (2.5 cm). Press, then stitch through all layers (fig. 4-26).

4. Mark quarter-points on skirt edge and deck edge.

5. Starting ¼″ (0.75 cm) from top edge and using the longest machine stitch, sew two rows of gathering threads ¼″ (0.75 cm) apart along top edge of skirt (fig. 4-27). Pull threads to gather skirt, gathering each section separately. In case threads break, it will be easier to regather one section rather than the entire skirt.

6. With right sides together, pin skirt to deck, matching quarter-points and arranging gathers evenly. Stitch in place, using gathering threads as a sewing guideline (fig. 4-28).

7. Topstitch seam allowance to deck from back, stitching next to seamline (fig. 4-29).

fig. 4-26   *fig. 4-27*

fig. 4-28   *fig. 4-29*

Tablecloth

8. Make a double-fold hem on all sides by turning up edge ¼″ (0.75 cm), then ¾″ (2 cm). Press, mitering corners. Stitch through all layers along foldline (fig. 4-30).

9. Add a tassel to each corner (fig. 4-31).

fig. 4-30

fig. 4-31

how to measure for tablecloth

For a circular table, make a square where each side is equal to tabletop diameter, plus 15″ (37.5 cm).

For a rectangular table, make a rectangle 8″ (20 cm) larger on all sides than tabletop.

tiny place mats and napkins

1. For each place mat, cut two rectangles, each 5½″ × 8½″ (13.75 cm × 21.25 cm). Use two different fabrics to make a reversible place mat.

2. Cut 5″ × 8″ (12.5 cm × 20 cm) fusible batting. Fuse to wrong side of place mat bottom.

3. Place right sides together (batting will be on outside). Stitch around outside edge, leaving a 3″ (7.5 cm) opening for turning. Clip corners; turn right side out (fig. 4-32).

4. Topstitch around all edges, closing opening at the same time. Topstitch again, approximately ¾″ (2 cm) away from all edges (fig. 4-33).

5. For each napkin, start with a 10″ × 10″ (25 cm × 25 cm) square.

6. Turn up ¾″ (2 cm) on edge; miter corners. Press.

7. Using machine buttonhole stitch, stitch along raw edge. For a hemstitched look, use constrasting thread and a wing needle or size 18 needle (fig 4-34).

fig. 4-32

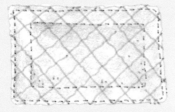

fig. 4-33

fig. 4-34

tea-time tuffet, tuffet skirt, and tuffet cushion

• •

Turn a sturdy plastic bucket upside down, cover it with a skirt, add a comfortable cushion, and it becomes a tiny tea-table tuffet.

Supplies

Fabric	Piece	Amount	Cut	Size
B	Tuffet skirt	¾ yd (0.75 m)	2	10¼″ × 30″ (25.5 cm × 75 cm)
A	Cushion top and bottom	½ yd (0.5 m)	2	9″ (22.5 cm) circle
C	Cushion sideband	⅛ yd (0.12 m)	1	3″ × 27¼″ (7.5 cm × 67.75 cm)
Bucket	Tuffet	2–3 gal (7.5–11 liter) sturdy plastic bucket		
Muslin	Tuffet deck	¼ yd (0.25 m)	1	9″ (22.5 cm) circle
1¼″ (3.25 cm) button			2	
¾″ (2 cm) Velcro		5″ (12.5 cm)	2	2½″ (6.25 cm)
Polyester fiber stuffing				

how to measure for skirt

Measure height of bucket. Measure circumference of bottom. Prepare a strip of fabric with a length equal to 2 to 2½ times the bottom circumference and a width equal to the bucket height plus 2″ (5 cm).

instructions

Use ½″ (1.25 cm) seam allowance unless otherwise noted.

Tuffet

1. Use a sturdy plastic bucket that holds 2 to 3 gallons (7.5 to 11 liters). Remove handle. Project shown uses a 2-gallon (7.5 liter) bucket with 8″ (20 cm) diameter bottom.

Tuffet Skirt

2. Follow directions for making Table Skirt, page 67

Tuffet Cushion

3. With right sides together, pin one end of side band to the other. Stitch; press seam open (fig. 4-35).

4. Mark quarter-points on side band, and on cushion top and bottom pieces.

5. With right sides together and matching raw edges, sandwich piping between cushion top and sideband, matching quarter-points. Pin carefully, easing cushion top to sideband at each quarter-point. Overlap ends of piping.

6. Using a zipper foot, stitch through all layers (fig. 4-36).

7. Join piping and sideband to cushion bottom as in Steps 3–4, but leave a 4″ (10 cm) opening for turning.

8. Clip curves; turn cushion right side out. Stuff (fig. 4-37). Close opening with ladder stitch (see page 119).

9. Center button on each side of cushion. Attach both buttons at same time by sewing through cushion. Pull buttons together while sewing to form a tuft on each side (fig. 4-38).

10. Use hand stitches to tack cushion to skirt. Use Velcro to attach skirt to overturned bucket.

how to measure for cushion

Cushion top and bottom: Trace around bottom of bucket on wrong side of fabric. Cut out, adding ½″ (1.25 cm) all around for seam allowance.
Cushion sideband: Length = diameter of bucket top/ bottom plus 1″ (2.5 cm); width = 3″ (7.5 cm).

fig. 4-35

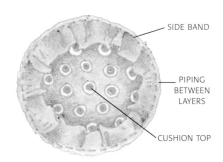

SIDE BAND

PIPING BETWEEN LAYERS

CUSHION TOP

fig. 4-36

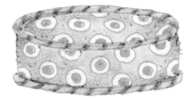

fig. 4-37

fig. 4-38

Make-Believe Adventures
Costumes for Dragon, Superhero, Robot, and Fairy

5

Watching children create lavish and complex imaginary worlds is a joy. There will be many adventures in Make-Believe Land with these grand costumes. All can be worn over leotard or play clothes.

fabric recommendations

See supplies chart for each costume.

costumes

Costumes are easy to make—it's the trims and appliqués that make them look complicated. Specific directions are given for each costume project, but the general procedure is as follows:

1. Fuse iron-on batting or interfacing to wrong side of costume fabric.
2. Attach appliqués to right side of costume fabric.
3. Attach Velcro if required.
4. With right sides together, stitch around outside edges.
5. Turn right side out and topstitch.

Costumes should be fun, so use sparkly, shiny fabrics. To make these fabrics easier to handle, try these ideas:

- Always use a pressing cloth when ironing costume fabrics.
- Interface lamé with iron-on tricot interfacing.
- Use pinking shears to finish raw edges and minimize raveling. Serge raw edges if raveling continues to be a problem.
- Felt is great for costumes because edges don't have to be finished.
- Fancy fabrics may shrivel and shrink if pressed with a hot iron, such as when pressing the fabric or fusing appliqués. Test scrap fabrics first.
- To make a better crease, as in hems or collars, use spray starch.
- Finish chiffon edges with lettuce edging (page 119).

dragon tabard

• •

The Dragon Tabard has scales on the front. There are wings and a spiny tail running down the back.

Supplies

Fabric	Piece	Amount	Cut	Size
70"- (175 cm-) wide felt	Tabard front/back/lining	¾ yd (0.75 m)	3	A × B
Felt	Tail		2	4" × 16" (10 cm × 40 cm)
Cotton	Wing	¾ yd (0.75 m)	2	See pattern
Cotton	Scales	½ yd (0.5 m)	40	4" × 4" (10 cm × 10 cm)
Cotton	Shoulder straps	¼ yd (0.25 m)	1	4" × 7" (10 cm × 17.5 cm)
	Side straps		1	4" × 10" (10 cm × 25 cm)
			2	3" × 7½" (7.5 cm × 18.75 cm)
Lightweight fusible interfacing	Straps	1 yd (1 m)	1	3½" × 6½" (8.75 cm × 16.25 cm)
			1	3½" × 9½" (8.75 cm × 23.75 cm)
			2	2½" × 7" (6.25 cm × 17.5 cm)
	Wing	1 yd (1 m)	1	See pattern
¾" (2 cm) Velcro		¼ yd (0.25 m)	3	1½" (4 cm) long
Fusible batting	Wing	¼ yd (0.25 m)		

measurements

A = across chest
B = clavicle to leg

instructions

Use ½" (1.25 cm) seam allowance unless otherwise noted. Patterns provided, beginning on page 127.

Make Tabard Front

1. Cut tabard front and front lining. Shape bottom corners (fig. 5-1).

fig. 5-1

2. Attach fuzzy Velcro on right side of front lining at waist and left shoulder as shown (fig. 5-2).

3. Pin fronts and front linings together, wrong sides facing. Topstitch around three sides, leaving top edge open (fig. 5-3). Clip curves; turn right side out.

4. Make dragon scale template from cardboard or template plastic.

5. For each dragon scale, place two 4″ (10 cm) squares right sides together. Center template and trace pattern on wrong side of one square. Stitch on this line, leaving an opening on top edge for turning. Make 20 scales.

6. Cut out scales, ¼″ (0.75 cm) from seamline (fig. 5-4). Clip curves; turn right side out. Press, turning top edge to inside.

7. Starting at bottom of tabard front, attach a staggered row of three scales. Stitch across top of scales through all layers. Add remaining scales in straight rows of two or three, as shown (fig. 5-5).

•option•

Make fierce-looking talons by gluing false fingernails to gloves. Glue pompoms to gloves to make spots on Dragon's paws.

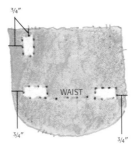

3/4″

WAIST

3/4″　　　　3/4″

fig. 5-2

fig. 5-3

fig. 5-4

how to make dragon scale template

1. Draw pattern on 4″ × 4″ (10 cm × 10 cm) grid.

2. Cut template.

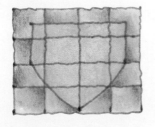

fig. 5-5

Add flash to costumes

- Sequins are sometimes dyed on one side only. If the non-dyed side is showing, color it with a marking pen.

- Attach strands of pearls with a beading foot and monofilament thread.

- To make ruffled lace, gather it by machine using a long stitch length and increasing tension on the top thread.

Make Tabard Back

8. To make tail, stack 4″ × 16″ (10 cm × 40 cm) felt tail pieces. Stitch two lines through all layers, then cut away excess fabric (fig. 5-6).

9. To make wing, fuse interfacing to wrong side of wing; fuse batting to wrong side of wing lining (fig. 5-7).

10. With right sides together, stitch around outside edge of wing, leaving an opening for turning (fig. 5-8). Clip curves. Turn right side out.

11. Topstitch around outside edges, closing opening. Add two more rows ¾″ from topstitched line and ¾″ (2 cm) apart (fig. 5-9).

12. Sandwich tail between two tabard backs, matching edges at center back. Top two spines are in seam; rest of tail hangs free. Stitch center back seam (fig. 5-10).

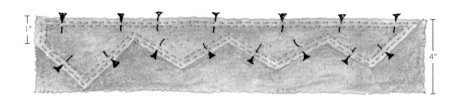

fig. 5-6

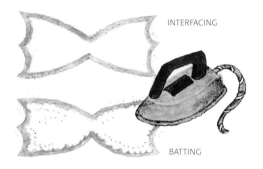

fig. 5-7

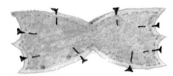

fig. 5-8

fig. 5-9

fig. 5-10

Make Straps

13. Fuse interfacing to wrong side of shoulder straps.

14. Fold each strap in half lengthwise, right sides together. Using ¼" (0.75 cm) seam, stitch along long edge of 4" × 7" (10 cm × 17.5 cm) strap; stitch long edge and one end of 4" × 10" (10 cm × 25 cm) strap (fig. 5-11).

15. Turn straps right side out. Topstitch along two long sides of 4" × 7" (10 cm × 17.5 cm) strap. Topstitch along three sides of 4" × 10" (10 cm × 25 cm) strap. Stitch Velcro to end of longer strap (fig. 5-12).

16. Repeat Steps 15–16 for side straps, except stitch Velcro to one end of each strap.

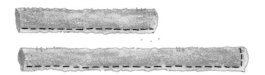

fig. 5-11

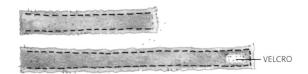

VELCRO

fig. 5-12

Assemble Tabard

17. Position back lining on tabard back, inserting side straps ½" (1.25 cm) between back and lining. Stitch around side and bottom edges, and next to center back seam (fig. 5-13).

18. Pin wing on tabard back. Stitch through all layers to hold (fig. 5-14).

19. Position shoulder straps inside tabard front and back. Topstitch to secure straps and close top edges (fig. 5-15).

fig. 5-13

fig. 5-14

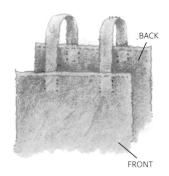

BACK

FRONT

fig. 5-15

dragon hood

Complete the Dragon costume with this easy-to-make hood. Ping-Pong ball eyes and a spine going down the center of the hood make an impressive disguise.

Supplies

Fabric	Piece	Amount	Cut	Size
Cotton	Right hood	½ yd (0.5 m)	1	See pattern
	Left hood		1	See pattern
	Chin strap		1	See pattern
Felt	Right hood lining	½ yd (0.5 m)	1	See pattern
	Left hood lining		1	See pattern
	Chin strap lining		1	3" × 7" (7.5 cm × 17.75 cm)
	Hood spine		2	3½" × 25" (8.75 cm × 62.5 cm)
Lightweight fusible interfacing	Hood, lining	1½ yd (1.4 m)	1 each	See pattern
	Chin strap			3" × 7" (7.5 cm × 17.75 cm)
Ping-Pong balls	Eyes	2		

Instructions

Use ½" (1.25 cm) seam allowance unless otherwise noted. Patterns are provided, beginning on page 127.

1. Cut hood, lining, chin strap, and chin strap lining.

2. Trim ½" (1.25 cm) off all sides of interfacing; fuse iron-on interfacing to wrong side of hood, lining, and chin strap pieces.

3. To make spine, stack 3½" × 25" (8.75 cm × 62.5 cm) felt spine pieces. Make pattern of seven or more spines. Stitch spines through all layers, then cut away excess fabric. Make two lines of stitching along all edges (fig. 5-16).

4. With right sides together, join chin tab to hood (fig. 5-17). Press seam open. Repeat for lining.

5. With right sides facing, pin hood lining pieces together. Sew center seam (fig. 5-18).

6. Repeat Step 4 for hood, except insert hood spine between hood layers, starting at top of hood (fig. 5-19).

7. Sew Velcro to right side of lining and hood (fig. 5-20).

8. Pin lining to hood, with right sides together and entire spine *inside* layers. Stitch around outside edges, leaving an opening on bottom edge for turning (fig. 5-21).

9. Clip curves, turn right side out. Topstitch around all edges, closing opening (fig. 5-22). For eyeballs, paint Ping-Pong balls. To sew eyeballs to hood, make four holes on bottom of each eye with large needle, and stitch as for buttons.

•tip•

When working with fabric that is the same on both sides—felt, for example—you will need to assign a "right" and "wrong" side and mark the fabric accordingly.

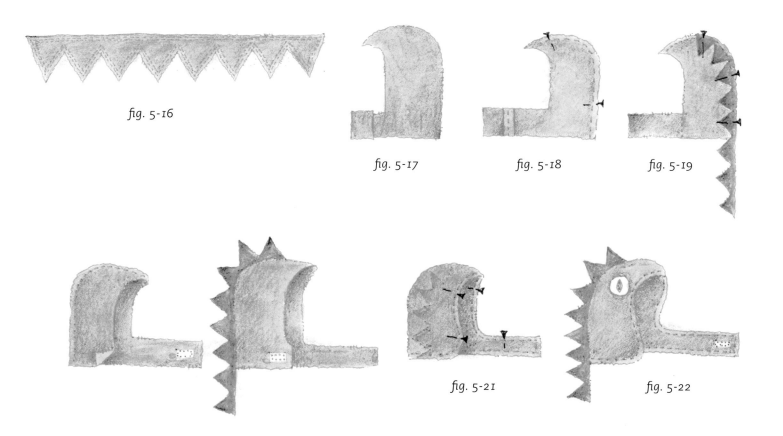

fig. 5-16

fig. 5-17

fig. 5-18

fig. 5-19

fig. 5-20

fig. 5-21

fig. 5-22

dragon spats

These easy-to-make spats have a spine and Velcro closure up the back; they fit over a child's shoes.

Supplies

Fabric	Piece	Amount	Cut	Size
Cotton	Spats	½ yd (0.5 m)	4	See Step 1
Felt	Lining	½ yd (0.5 m)	4	See Step 1
Felt	Spine		4	2″ × 6″ (5 cm × 15 cm)
¼″ (0.75 cm) elastic	10″ (25 cm)	2	5″ (12.5 cm)	
Lightweight fusible interfacing	Spats	¾ yd (0.75 m)	4	See Step 1
Fusible batting	Spats	12″ × 25″ (30 cm × 62.5 cm)	2	See Step 1
¾″ (2 cm) Velcro	10″ (25 cm)	2	5″ (12.5 cm)	

measurements

A = calf ÷ 2 + 2″ (5 cm)

B = shoe circumference ÷ 2 + 2″ (5 cm)

C = midcalf to floor

D = over arch ÷ 2 + 2″ (5 cm)

E = over toe ÷ 2 + 2″ (5 cm)

instructions

Use ½″ (1.25 cm) seam allowance unless otherwise noted.

1. Make pattern, following diagram carefully (fig. 5-23). Cut out spats, lining, interfacing, and batting.

2. Trim ½″ (1.25 cm) off all sides of interfacing; fuse iron-on interfacing to wrong side of spats. Trim ½″ (1.25 cm) off all sides of batting; fuse batting to wrong side of spat linings.

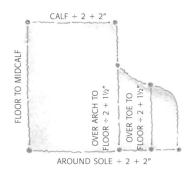
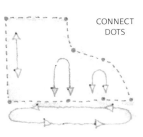

fig. 5-23

3. With right sides together, pin one spat onto another to make two spats. Sew center front seams (fig. 5-24). Clip curves and turn right side out.

4. Repeat Step 3 for spat linings.

5. Attach fuzzy Velcro to right side of linings and attach hook Velcro to right sides of spats (fig. 5-25). Note differences for right and left feet.

6. To make *each* spine, stack two pieces of felt. Cut four notches along one edge. Make two lines of stitching along all edges (fig. 5-26).

7. Pin linings to spats, right sides together. Sandwich spines inside ends with Velcro on lining. Sandwich elastic between lining and spat on bottom edge. Stitch around all edges, leaving open the end with no spine. (fig. 5-27).

8. Clip curves; turn right side out. Topstitch to close opening.

•tip•

Follow placement diagrams carefully. Spats are designed for right and left feet.

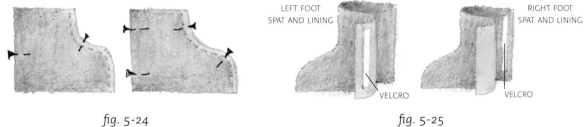

fig. 5-24

LEFT FOOT
SPAT AND LINING

VELCRO

RIGHT FOOT
SPAT AND LINING

VELCRO

fig. 5-25

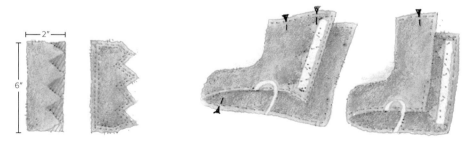

fig. 5-26

fig. 5-27

superhero/robot reversible tabard

•••

Change characters by reversing this simple tabard. Superhero motifs are on one side; Robot motifs are on the reverse. Superhero has a detachable cape, too.

Supplies

Fabric	Piece	Amount	Cut	Size
Taffeta	Tabard front and back (Superhero)	½ yd (0.5 m)	2	A × B
Lamé	Tabard front and back (Robot)	½ yd (0.5 m)	2	A × B
Taffeta	Cape (Superhero)		1	17″ × 28″ (42.5 cm × 70 cm)
Taffeta	Shoulder straps		2	5″ × 7″ (12.5 cm × 17.5 cm)
			1	5″ × 3″ (12.5 cm × 7.5 cm)
Cotton	Side straps		2	2½″ × 7″ (6.25 cm × 17.5 cm)
Lightweight fusible interfacing	Straps	1½ yd (1.4 m)	2	4″ × 6″ (10 cm × 15 cm)
			1	4″ × 2″ (10 cm × 5 cm)
			2	2″ × 6″ (5 cm × 15 cm)
	Tabard		4	A × B
Fusible batting	Tabard	30″ × 30″ (75 cm × 75 cm)	4	A × B
Velcro		6″ (15 cm)		
½″ (1.25 cm) buttons		2		
1½″ (3.75 cm) buttons		2		

measurements

A = across chest + 1″ (2.5 cm)
B = clavicle to leg + 1″ (2.5 cm)

how to cut triangle motifs

Use squares as shown to cut perfect equilateral triangles.

Motifs

Fabric	Piece	Amount	Cut	Size
Cotton	Wide vertical stripe (back)		1	2″ (5 cm) × B
Cotton	Horizontal stripe (back)		1	1″ (2.5 cm) × A
Cotton	Horizontal stripe (front)		1	2″ (5 cm) × A
Taffeta	Narrow vertical stripe (back)		1	1″ (2.5 cm) × B
Cotton	Flame	6″ × 8″ (15 cm × 20 cm)	1	See pattern
Taffeta	Emblem	5″ × 6″ (12.5 cm × 15 cm)	1	See pattern
Cotton	Initial	3″ × 3″ (7.5 cm × 7.5 cm)	1	See pattern
Taffeta	Triangle	4″ × 4″ (10 cm × 10 cm)	1	See page 82
Taffeta	Triangle	2″ × 2″ (5 cm × 5 cm)	1	See page 82
Taffeta	Rectangle	Scrap	1	1″ × 2″ (2.5 cm × 5 cm)
Cotton	Circle	Scrap	5	1″ (2.5 cm) circle

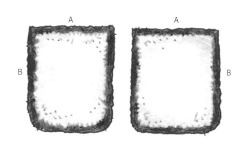

fig. 5-28

instructions

Use ½″ (1.25 cm) seam allowance unless otherwise noted. Patterns are provided, beginning on page 127.

Make Superhero Front and Back

1. Cut Superhero front, Superhero back, interfacing, and batting.

2. Fuse interfacing to wrong side of tabard front and back. Fuse batting to wrong side of tabard front and back. Round off bottom corners (fig. 5-28).

3. Prepare all appliqués (page 115). Arrange as shown in fig. 5-38.

4. Iron paper-backed-fusible adhesive to horizontal belt. Cut belt as shown (fig. 5-29).

5. Fuse initial to emblem, then position emblem and flame on tabard front. Add horizontal belt.

6. Secure edges of flame with free-motion stitching. Satin stitch around emblem and initial. Use decorative stitch on edges of stripe. Stitch two quilting lines and add button trim, as shown (fig. 5-30).

fig. 5-29

fig. 5-30

Make Robot Front and Back

7. Cut Robot front, Robot back, interfacing, and batting.

8. Fuse interfacing to wrong side of tabard front and back. Fuse batting to wrong side of tabard front and back. Round off bottom corners, as in Step 1.

9. Cut 2″ (5 cm) and 4″ (10 cm) triangles. Prepare all appliqués (see page 115).

Appliqué Robot Front and Back

10. Fuse smaller shapes to larger rectangles.

11. Arrange shapes on front, then fuse (fig. 5-31).

12. Use free-motion machine stitch to secure motifs. Use satin stitch or decorative stitch to secure edges of larger appliqués (fig. 5-32).

13. Fuse large triangle to back. Satin stitch around edges. Add quilting lines (fig. 5-33).

ROBOT FRONT

fig. 5-31

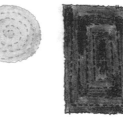 

fig. 5-32

ROBOT BACK

fig. 5-33

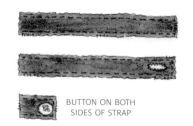

BUTTON ON BOTH
SIDES OF STRAP

fig. 5-34

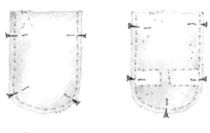

fig. 5-35

Make Straps

14. Fuse iron-on interfacing to wrong side of shoulder straps.

15. Fold each strap in half lengthwise, right sides together. Stitch along raw edges of each strap. Stitch across short end of one 5″ × 7″ (12.5 cm × 17.5 cm) strap and the 5″ × 3″ (12.5 cm × 7.5 cm) strap. Turn straps right side out.

16. Topstitch long sides of one 5″ × 7″ (12.5 cm × 17.5 cm) strap; topstitch three sides of one 5″ × 7″ (12.5 cm × 17.5 cm) strap and 5″ × 3″ (12.5 cm × 7.5 cm) strap (fig. 5-34).

17. Sew 1½″ (3.75 cm) button on both sides of 5″ × 3″ (12.5 cm × 7.5 cm) strap. Make buttonhole on end of 5″ × 7″ (12.5 cm × 17.5 cm) strap with closed end (fig. 5-34).

18. Make two 2½″ × 7″ (6.25 cm × 17.5 cm) side straps in the same manner as 5″ × 7″ (12.5 cm × 17.5 cm) straps, including buttonholes to fit ½″ (1.25 cm) buttons (fig. 5-35).

Assemble Tabard

19. With right sides together, pin Superhero front to Robot front. Stitch around three sides, leaving top edge open (fig. 5-36). Clip curves; turn right side out.

20. Pin side straps to waist on right side of Superhero back, matching raw edges. With right sides together, pin Superhero back to Robot back, keeping straps inside. With right sides together, place Superhero back on Robot back, keeping side straps inside. Stitch around three sides, leaving top edge open (fig. 5-37). Clip curves, turn right side out.

21. Fold top edges of tabards to inside. Position shoulder straps and shoulder tab inside top edges (fig. 5-38). Topstitch to secure straps and close opening.

22. Attach ½″ (1.25 cm) buttons to Superhero front at belt.

fig. 5-36   *fig.* 5-37

fig. 5-38

Make Superhero Cape

23. Fold over bottom edge ¼″ (0.75 cm), then ¼″ (0.75 cm) again, forming a double-fold hem. Repeat for side edges.

24. Stitch gathering thread across top edge. Pull thread and gather to 7″ (17.5 cm) wide. Fuse interfacing to wrong side of band.

25. With right sides up, pin cape to band, matching raw edges. Stitch through all layers (fig. 5-39).

26. Press band away from cape, then fold over top edge of band ¼″ (0.75 cm); press (fig. 5-40).

27. Fold band to front of cape, covering raw edges and gathering stitches; fold ends of band to inside. Topstitch from front through all layers, closing band ends (fig. 5-41).

28. Sew hook Velcro to back of band (fig. 5-42). To attach cape, stitch fuzzy Velcro to tabard back, 1″ (2.5 cm) from top edge.

•option•

Make individual tabards for Superhero and Robot, if desired. Use a solid-colored fabric as the lining.

fig. 5-39

fig. 5-40

fig. 5-41

fig. 5-42

superhero/robot gauntlets
• •

These reversible gauntlets are great costume accessories. One side is for Superhero, the other is for Robot.

Supplies

Fabric	Piece	Amount	Cut	Size
Taffeta	Superhero gauntlet	½ yd (0.5 m)	4	See Step 1
Lamé	Robot gauntlet	½ yd (0.5 m)	4	See Step 1
Felt	Flame extension	1½" × 6" (3.75 cm × 15 cm)	2	1½" × 3" (3.75 cm × 7.5 cm)
Lightweight fusible interfacing		½ yd (0.5 m)	4	See Step 1
Fusible batting		15" × 20" (37.5 cm × 50 cm)	4	See Step 1
Velcro		5" (12.5 cm)	2	2½" (6.25 cm)
Motifs				
Taffeta	Emblem		2	See pattern
Cotton	Triangle	2" × 2" (5 cm × 5 cm)	2	See page 82

measurements

A = wrist + 2½" (6.25 cm)
B = forearm + 2½" (6.25 cm)
C = wrist to forearm + 1" (2.5 cm)

instructions

Use ½" (1.25 cm) seam allowance unless otherwise noted. Patterns are provided, beginning on page 127.

1. Make pattern, following diagram carefully (fig. 5-43). Gauntlets are designed for right and left hands. Cut two Superhero gauntlets and two Robot gauntlets.

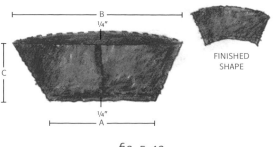

fig. 5-43

2. Fuse iron-on interfacing to wrong side of all gauntlets. Fuse iron-on batting to wrong side of all gauntlets.

3. Attach Velcro to right side of each gauntlet. Sew fuzzy Velcro to Superhero gauntlet; sew hook Velcro to Robot gauntlet (fig. 5-44).

4. Prepare appliqués (page 115). Fuse to gauntlets (fig. 5-45). Secure outside edges of appliqués with satin stitch.

5. For gauntlet extension, stack 1½" × 3" (3.75 cm × 7.5 cm) felt pieces, then trim along one edge to make a flame shape (fig. 5-46).

6. Place righthand gauntlets together, right sides facing, keeping felt flame to inside. Insert flame extension at same end as hook Velcro. Stitch around outside edges, leaving opposite end open for turning. Repeat for lefthand gauntlet (fig. 5-47). Clip corners, turn right side out.

7. Topstitch around outside edges, closing opening (fig. 5-48). Flame will tuck to inside when Robot gauntlets are worn.

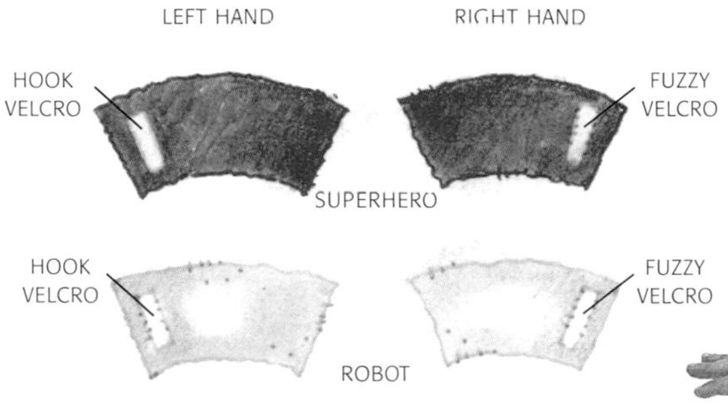

fig. 5-44

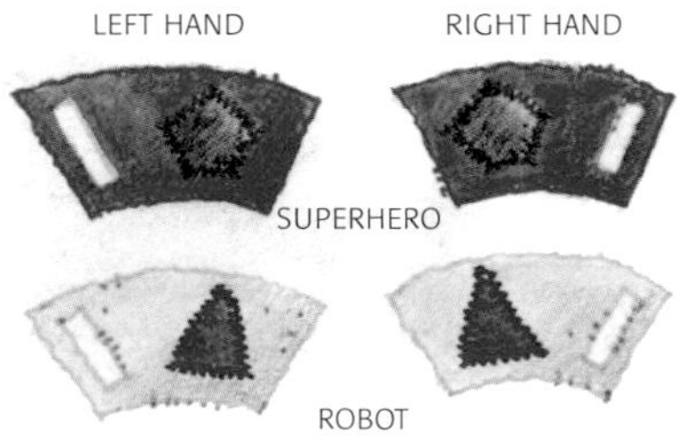

fig. 5-45

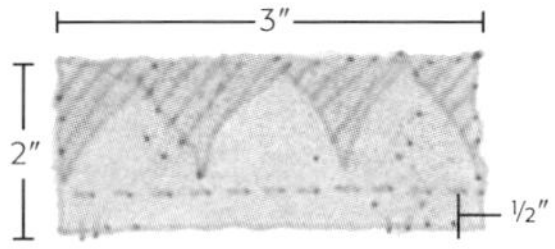

fig. 5-46

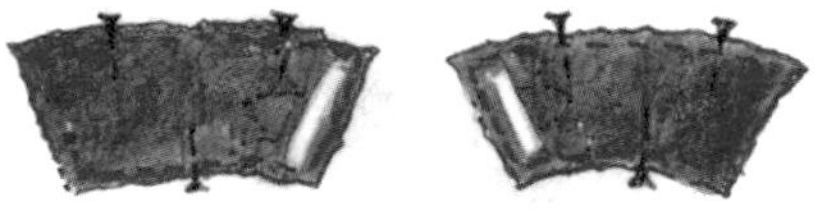

fig. 5-47

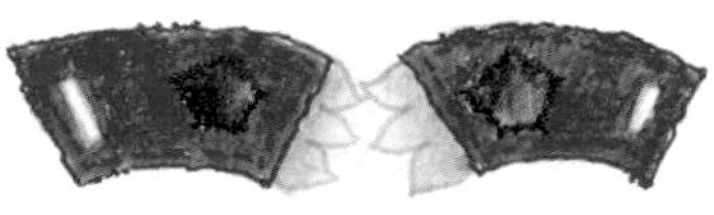

fig. 5-48

superhero/robot spats

● ●

Reversible spats fit over shoes. Motifs reverse from Superhero to Robot.

Supplies

Fabric	Piece	Amount	Cut	Size
Taffeta	Superhero spat	½ yd (0.5 m)	4	See Step 1
Lamé	Robot spat	½ yd (0.5 m)	4	See Step 1
Mesh	Robot overlay	½ yd (0.5 m)	4	See Step 1
Lightweight fusible interfacing		1½ yd (1.4 m)	4	See Step 1
Lightweight fusible batting		30″ × 36″ (75 cm × 90 cm)	4	See Step 1
¼″ (0.75 cm) elastic		10″ (25 cm)	2	5″ (12.5 cm)
¾″ (2 cm) Velcro		10″ (25 cm)	2	5″ (12.5 cm)
Motifs				
Taffeta	Emblem	5″ × 6″ (12.5 cm × 15 cm)	2	See pattern
Cotton	Flame	6″ × 8″ (15 cm × 20 cm)	2	See pattern
Cotton	Triangle	2″ × 2″ (5 cm × 5 cm)	2	See page 82
Taffeta	Rectangle	Scrap	2	1½″ × 2¾″ (3.75 cm × 7 cm)
Cotton		Scrap	4	1″ (2.5 cm) circles

instructions

Use ½″ (1.25 cm) seam allowance unless otherwise noted. Patterns are provided, beginning on page 127.

1. Make pattern as for Dragon spats (page 80). Cut two Superhero spats and two Robot spats.

2. Fuse interfacing to wrong side of all spats. Fuse batting to wrong sides of all spats.

3. Prepare appliqués; fuse to spats as shown (fig. 5-49). Secure outside edges of appliqués with satin stitches or free-motion stitching (page 118), as on tabard.

4. Sew mesh overlay to Robot spats, stitching inside seam allowance. Stitch around appliqués (fig. 5-50).

5. Finish spats as for Dragon spats, Steps 3–7, treating Superhero side as the lining.

•option•

Make a hood for the robot costume using the instructions for the Dragon Hood. Omit the spine, and fuse robot motifs to lamé before sewing mesh overlay.

SUPERHERO   ROBOT

fig. 5-49   *fig. 5-50*

•option•

Every Superhero has an identity to conceal. Make a simple mask by gluing felt shapes to inexpensive sunglasses.

fairy wings

Fairies need wings to flit happily about while they play. These wings can be attached with safety pins or Velcro.

Supplies

Fabric	Piece	Amount	Cut	Size
Lamé	Wings	½ yd (0.5 m)	2	See pattern
Sequined fabric	Spots on wings	10" × 10" (25 cm × 25 cm)	4	See pattern
Fusible interfacing		¾ yd (0.75 m)	2	See pattern
Fusible batting		6" × 9" (15 cm × 22.5 cm)	1	See pattern
¾" (2 cm) Velcro		3" (7.5 cm)		

instructions

Use ½" (1.25 cm) seam allowance unless otherwise noted. Patterns are provided, beginning on page 127.

1. Fuse iron-on interfacing to wrong side of wing fabric. Using pattern, cut wings and batting.

2. Prepare appliqué spots (page 115). Position on front wing, then fuse (fig. 5-51).

3. On batting, trim ½" (1.25 cm) all around. Fuse to wrong side of wing back. Stitch hook Velcro to center of wing back on right side (fig. 5-52).

4. With right sides together, join wing front to wing back. Stitch around outside edges, leaving a 4" (10 cm) opening for turning (fig. 5-53). Clip curves; turn right side out.

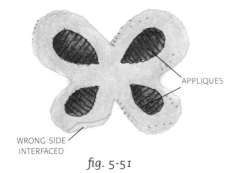

APPLIQUES

WRONG SIDE
INTERFACED

fig. 5-51

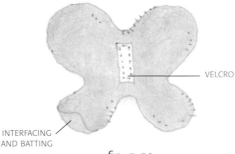

VELCRO

INTERFACING
AND BATTING

fig. 5-52

fig. 5-53

5. Topstitch around all edges, closing opening. Using machine straight stitch, secure appliqués by sewing along edge through all layers (fig. 5-54). Stitch fuzzy Velcro to leotard; attach wings.

fig. 5-54

fairy collar

You will need ¼ yard (0.25 m) of sequined fabric, plus the same amount of taffeta for lining. You will also need ½ yard (0.5 m) lightweight fusible interfacing and 2½″ (6.25 cm) of ¾″ (2 cm) Velcro. Fuse interfacing to wrong side of collar fabric. Using patterns on page 143, cut one collar front and two collar backs from fused fabric and from lining. Position Velcro outside seam allowance on corners of back collar and lining. Stitch to secure. Right sides together, pin collar to lining. Stitch around outside edges, leaving opening for turning. Clip curves, trim off corners; turn right side out. Press. Turn raw edges to inside and stitch opening closed.

measurements

A = waist + 1″ (2.5 cm)

fairy petal skirt

This quick-and-easy Fairy Petal Skirt is perfect for dancing and twirling. Layers of petal shapes are attached to a waistband.

Supplies

Fabric	Piece	Amount	Cut	Size
Poly silk	Waistband	1/8 yd (0.15 m)	1	4″ × 44″ (10 cm × 110 cm)
Organza		1/2 yd (0.5 m)	4	11″ × 12″ (27.5 cm × 30 cm)
Organza		1/2 yd (0.5 m)	4	11″ × 12″ (27.5 cm × 30 cm)
Tulle		1/2 yd (0.5 m)	8	11″ × 12″ (27.5 cm × 30 cm)
1″ (2.5 cm) elastic	A			

•tip•

For lettuce edge, set machine to short stitch length and narrow zigzag, so that left swing of needle is in fabric and right swing is just off fabric. The zigzag stitch will roll and whip the edge of the fabric while sewing. To ruffle the edge, gently stretch the fabric (in front of needle only) during stitching process.

instructions

Use 1/2″ (1.25 cm) seam allowance unless otherwise noted.

1. Cut 16 petal shapes as shown (fig. 5-55).
2. Make a lettuce edge on sides and bottom of each petal, except for tulle petals. This will give petals a soft, ruffled edge (fig. 5-56).
3. Pin four tulle petals to waistband, matching raw edges (fig. 5-57).

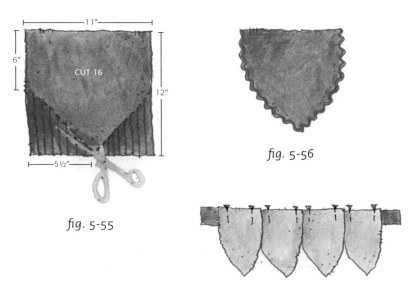

fig. 5-55

fig. 5-56

fig. 5-57

4. Pin four lettuced organza petals to waistband, overlapping and staggering points (fig. 5-58).

5. Pin two more layers of petals on waistband as in Steps 3–4.

6. Stitch through all layers to secure petals to waistband (fig. 5-59).

7. Press waistband seam. Fold over top edge of waistband ½″ (1.25 cm) (fig. 5-60); press.

8. With right sides together, join ends of waistband.

9. Fold waistband over raw edges to front of skirt. Topstitch through all layers, leaving an opening for elastic (fig. 5-61).

10. Insert elastic into casing; overlap ends and stitch. Close opening (fig. 5-62).

•tip•

When collecting fabrics for Fairy costume, include light and dark organza and light and dark tulle. Varying the color and value adds interest and pizzazz to the finished project.

fig. 5-58

fig. 5-59

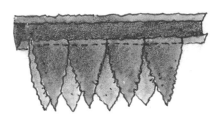

fig. 5-60

fig. 5-61

fig. 5-62

fairy petal bracelets

Little fairies love to adorn themselves with pretty accessories. Make these delightful Fairy Petal Bracelets for wrists and ankles.

Supplies

Fabric	Amount	Cut	Size
Wrist Petals			
Organza	¼ yd (0.25 m)	2	5″ × 14″ (12.5 cm × 35 cm)
Organza	¼ yd (0.25 m)	2	3″ × 14″ (7.5 cm × 35 cm)
Tulle	¼ yd (0.25 m)	4	3″ × 14″ (7.5 cm × 35 cm)
¼″ (0.75 cm) elastic	1 yd (1 m)	2	A
Ankle Petals			
Organza		2	5″ × 20″ (12.5 cm × 50 cm)
Organza		2	3″ × 20″ (7.5 cm × 50 cm)
Tulle		4	3″ × 20″ (7.5 cm × 50 cm)
¼″ (0.75 cm) elastic	1 yd (1 m)	2	B

measurements

A = wrist + 1½″ (3.75 cm)
B = ankle + 1½″ (3.75 cm)

instructions

Use ½″ (1.25 cm) seam allowance unless otherwise noted. Fairy Petal Bracelets for wrists and ankles are identical except for length of petal strips.

1. Make 2″ (5 cm) accordion folds on each fabric strip and cut as shown (figs. 5-63a, b, and c).

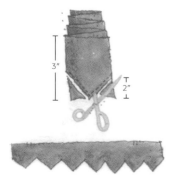

fig. 5-63a

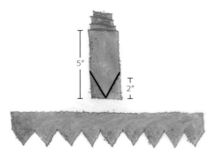

fig. 5-63b

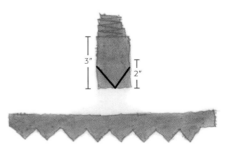

fig. 5-63c

2. Make lettuce edgings (page 119) around all points, except on tulle strips. Straighten out inside points while sewing; round off outside points. Points will have a soft, rounded edge.

fig. 5-64

3. Stack narrow layers on top of widest layer, as shown; starting from bottom, stack organza, tulle, organza, tulle. Points will overlap. Stitch through all layers (fig. 5-64).

4. With right sides together, stitch across ends to make a circle (fig. 5-65).

5. Fold over top edge ½″ (1.25 cm) (fig. 5-66), then fold to cover raw edges and form casing.

6. Topstitch, leaving an opening for elastic (fig. 5-67). Insert elastic; overlap ends and stitch. Close opening.

fig. 5-65

fig. 5-66

fig. 5-67

fairy petal flowers

Use these flowers as trims on fairy accessories. For added interest, mix light and dark colors.

1. Cut 3″ × 18″ (7.5 cm × 45 cm) strips of organza.
2. Prepare strips as in Steps 1–2 for bracelets. These strips can be gathered and attached as trims as for Fairy Wand (page 99).
3. Stack two strips, one atop another, raw edges matching.
4. Sew gathering thread across straight edges through all layers (fig. 5-68).
5. Pull thread to gather; lockstitch to hold (fig. 5-69).

fig. 5-68

fig. 5-69

fairy wreath

Fairies need lovely wreaths for their hair with streamers trailing down their backs. This Fairy Wreath is trimmed with ribbons, pearls, and Fairy Petal Flowers.

Supplies

Fabric	Amount	Cut	Size
Polyester silk	⅛ yd (0.12 m)	4	4″ × 44″ (10 cm × 110 cm)
Organza Fairy Petal Flowers (page 97)		2	
¾″ (2 cm) cord	1¼ yd (1.2 m)	2	Head circumference less 1″ (2.5 cm)
Duct tape			

instructions

Use ½″ (1.25 cm) seam allowance unless otherwise noted.

1. Place two lengths of cord together and wrap with duct tape (fig. 5-70).

2. Fold silk strip in half lengthwise, matching long edges, wrong side out. Stitch along long edge, forming a tube.

3. Turn tube right side out. Insert wrapped cord. Butt ends of cord and cover with tape.

4. Fold one end of tube to inside. Insert opposite end into tube opening. Close tube ends with invisible hand stitches.

5. Wrap ribbons and pearls around tube. Hand stitch ends to tube; begin and end at seamline.

6. For streamers, cut 5–9 pieces of ribbon, each 18″–25″ (45 cm–62.5 cm) long. Fold in half to make a variety of lengths.

7. Hand stitch two Fairy Petal Flowers (page 97) to band on top of ribbon streamers.

fig. 5-70

fairy wand

Good little fairies keep their magic wands handy. A sparkly star tops this Fairy Wand.

Supplies

Fabric	Piece	Amount	Cut	Size
Sequined fabric	Star	9″ × 9″ (22.5 cm × 22.5 cm)	2	See pattern
Lightweight interfacing		8″ × 8″ (20 cm × 20 cm)	2	8″ × 8″ (20 cm × 20 cm)
Assorted trims and acrylic paint				
¼″ (0.75 cm) dowel rod		13″ (32.5 cm) long		
Wooden knobs with ¼″ (0.75 cm) hole		2		

instructions

1. Trace star shape onto one piece of interfacing. Fuse interfacing to wrong side of fabric squares (fig. 5-71).

2. With right sides together, place one star fabric on another. Sew slightly outside traced line, leaving an opening for turning (fig. 5-72).

3. Cut out star. Clip curves and corners; turn right side out. Stuff points of star.

4. Prepare dowel: Put glue in knob holes, then insert dowel. After glue has dried, paint dowel and knobs. Wrap ribbons and pearls around dowel and secure with glue (fig. 5-73).

5. Make streamers. For streamers, cut 5–9 pieces of ribbon, each 18″–25″ (45 cm–62.5 cm) long. Fold in half to make a variety of lengths. Tack together at centerpoint. Using hot glue, attach to top knob. Insert dowel into star. Finish stuffing. Close opening around dowel rod with ladder stitch (page 119).

6. Using three to four 30″ (75 cm) lengths of ribbon, tie bow at bottom of dowel. Secure with hot glue.

fig. 5-71

fig. 5-72

PAINT

GLUE

PEARLS

fig. 5-73

RIBBON

Travel Time
Accessories for Vacations and Overnights

Toddlers are good little travelers, especially when they have their own tote bag to carry. A soft flannel Teddy Bear Quilt and matching pillow are handy for a comfy ride. Traveling Teddy, a velveteen bear, is nice and cuddly, so napping is easier when your toddler is away from home. Hang the Car Organizer on the back of the front seat. See-through vinyl pockets keep treasures in sight and in order.

fabric recommendations

Flannel

Extra-soft pinwale corduroy

Quilt cottons

Velveteen

Projects shown use eight coordinating fabrics

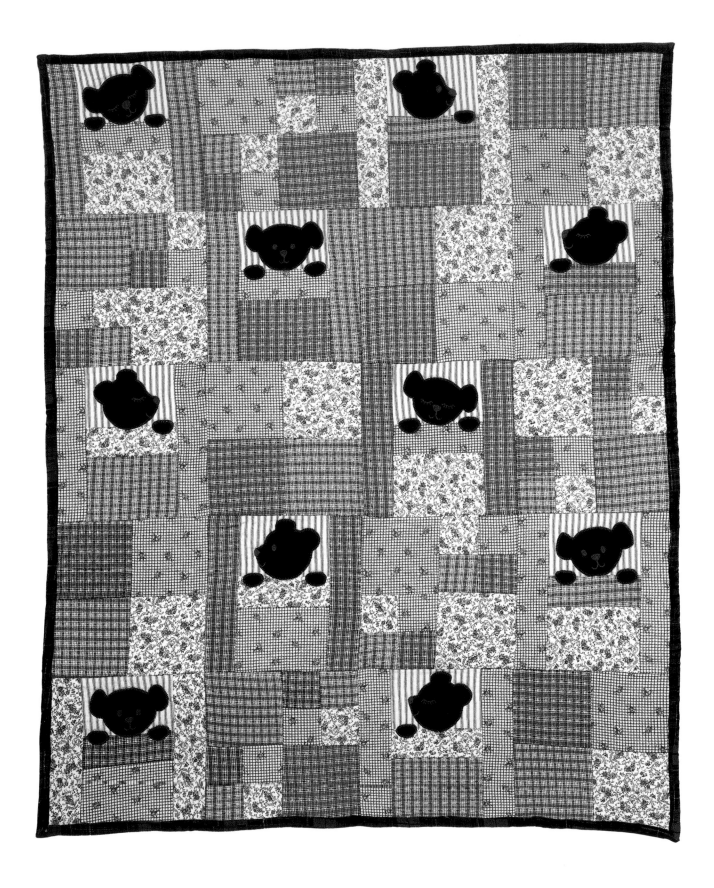

teddy bear quilt

• •

Wrap this snuggly flannel quilt around your toddler to make it easier to sleep while traveling. The little teddy bears appliquéd on the quilt are settling down for a nap, too. Three blocks are used: Four-Patch, Double Four-Patch, and Teddy Bear. Finished size is 40″ × 50″ (100 cm × 125 cm).

•tip•

After cutting strips, pin them together and mark sizes on each set of strips.

Supplies

Fabric	Piece	Amount	Cut	Size
A	Red plaid	¾ yd (0.75 m)	2	3″ × 44″ (7.5 cm × 110 cm)
			2	5½″ × 44″ (13.75 cm × 110 cm)
			3	2½″ × 44″ (6.25 cm × 110 cm)
			3	4½″ × 6½″ (11.25 cm × 16.25 cm)
B	Green plaid	¾ yd (0.75 m)	2	3″ × 44″ (7.5 cm × 110 cm)
			2	5½″ × 44″ (13.75 cm × 110 cm)
			3	2½″ × 44″ (6.25 cm × 110 cm)
			3	4½″ × 6½″ (11.25 cm × 16.25 cm)
C	Red flower	¾ yd (0.75 m)	2	3″ × 44″ (7.5 cm × 110 cm)
			2	5½″ × 44″ (13.75 cm × 110 cm)
			3	2½″ × 44″ (6.25 cm × 110 cm)
			3	4½″ × 6½″ (11.25 cm × 16.25 cm)
D	Green flower	¾ yd (0.75 m)	2	3″ × 44″ (7.5 cm × 110 cm)
			2	5½″ × 44″ (13.75 cm × 110 cm)
			3	2½″ × 44″ (6.25 cm × 110 cm)
			3	4½″ × 6½″ (11.25 cm × 16.25 cm)
E	Ticking	½ yd (0.25 m)	11	4½″ × 6½″ (11.25 cm × 16.25 cm)
F	Velveteen bears and paws	½ yd (0.5 m)		See pattern
	Backing	1½ yd (1.4 m)		
	Batting			45″ × 60″ (112.5 cm × 150 cm) (crib size)

instructions

Use ¼" (0.75 cm) seam allowance unless otherwise noted. Patterns are provided, beginning on page 127.

Double Four-Patch Block

1. Cut one 5½" (13.75 cm) block from each 5½" × 44" (13.75 cm × 110 cm) strip. Cut another block from any two strips. You now have ten squares, each 5½" × 5½" (13.75 cm × 13.75 cm), as shown (fig. 6-1).

2. Sew together two 3" × 44" (7.5 cm × 110 cm) strips to make four strip sets; press seam toward darker fabric. Cut five 3" (7.5 cm) strips from these sets, as shown. Arrange randomly to make ten Four-Patch blocks (fig. 6-2). Press seams.

3. Combine single squares and Four-Patch blocks to make five Double Four-Patch blocks (fig. 6-3). Press.

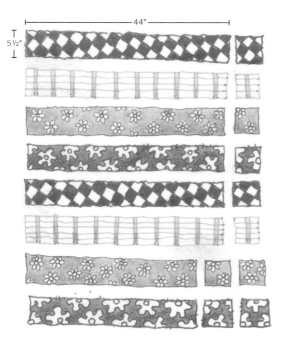

fig. 6-1

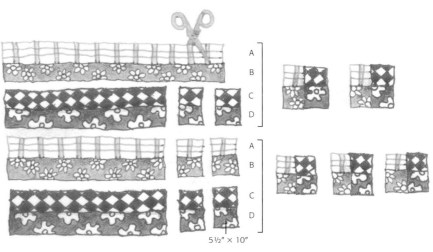

fig. 6-2

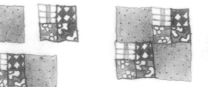

fig. 6-3

Four-Patch Block

4. Sew together any two 5½″ (13.75 cm) strips to make four strip sets. Cut ten 5½″ (13.75 cm) strips from these sets.

5. Randomly arrange to make five Four-Patch blocks (fig. 6-4). Press.

Teddy Bear Block

6. Sew together 4½″ × 6½″ (11.25 cm × 16.25 cm) ticking, any narrow 2½″ × 6½″ (6.25 cm × 16.25 cm) strip, and any 4½″ × 6½″ (11.25 cm × 16.25 cm) rectangle (fig. 6-5). Press seams toward middle strip.

7. Add matching 2½″ (6.25 cm) strips along each outside edge by sewing, then cut off excess (fig. 6-6). Open and press. Make nine more blocks.

8. Prepare bear and paw appliqués (see page 115). Trace appliqué design onto paper backing of fusible adhesive. Reverse the side-view bear so that you will have two facing one direction and three facing the other.

9. Fuse adhesive to wrong side of bear fabric. Cut out bears and paws and peel away backing. Position bears and paws. Fuse in place (fig. 6-7).

10. Outline bears and paws with machine buttonhole stitch. Stitch facial details using free-motion machine stitching (page 117) (fig. 6-8).

•tip•

Use removable stabilizer under fabric when embroidering bears. When stitching is completed, gently tear off stabilizer while holding onto stitches.

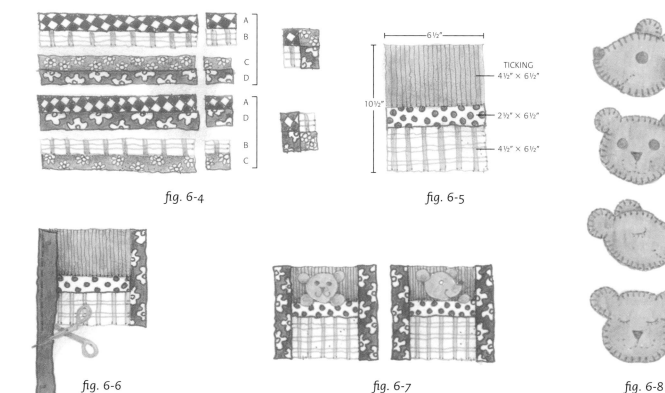

fig. 6-4

fig. 6-5

fig. 6-6

fig. 6-7

fig. 6-8

fig. 6-9

fig. 6-10

•option•

For traditional binding you'll need 6 yards (5.5 m) of extra-wide double-fold bias tape.

Assemble Quilt

11. Square up blocks, using ruler and rotary cutter.

12. Arrange blocks as shown. Sew blocks together across rows, then join rows (fig. 6-9). Press each seam after it is sewn.

13. Square up quilt top, using ruler and rotary cutter.

14. Layer backing, batting, and quilt top. Baste layers together (see page 121).

15. Quilt along all seam lines. Quilt around bear heads and paws (fig. 6-10).

16. Trim backing and batting to 1¼″ (3.12 cm) around all edges. Trim batt to ¼″ (0.75 cm) (fig. 6-11).

17. To make self-binding, fold backing to front, turning up edges ¼″ (0.75 cm), then ¾″ (2 cm). Fold sides first, then top and bottom. Fold corners at angle to miter. Stitch along edge through all layers (fig. 6-12).

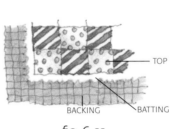

fig. 6-11

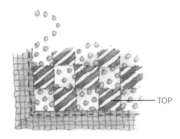

fig. 6-12

travel pillow

Use extra squares from the Car Quilt to make a travel pillow.

1. Join four 5½″ (13.75 cm) squares to make a four-patch block. Add 2½″ (6.25 cm) border strips along the outside edges.

2. Cut backing 14½″ × 14½″ (36.25 cm × 36.25 cm). Pin to front, right sides together.

3. Sew around outside edges, leaving a 6″ (15 cm) opening for turning. Clip corners.

4. Turn right side out. Insert pillow form. Close opening with ladder stitch.

travel tote

Make a special tote for overnight visits. It's easy to make and just the right size for toothbrush, pajamas, a change of clothes, and bedtime storybook. Finished size is 10" high × 10" wide × 6" deep (25 cm high × 25 cm wide × 15 cm deep).

Supplies

Fabric	Piece	Amount	Cut	Size
G	Tote	½ yd (0.5 m)	2	Each, 14" × 17" (35 cm × 42.5 cm)
A	Lining	½ yd (0.5 m)	2	Each, 14" × 17" " (35 cm × 42.5 cm)
G	Strap		1	3" × 28" (7.5 cm × 70 cm)
G	Flap		1	6" × 9" (15 cm × 22.5 cm)
A	Flap lining		1	6" × 9" (15 cm × 22.5 cm)
	Appliqué	8" × 8" (20 cm × 20 cm)		See pattern
	Interfacing	1 yd (1 m)	1	13½" × 16½" (33.75 cm × 41.25 cm)
			1	2½" × 27" (6.25 cm × 67.5 cm)

instructions

Use ½" (1.25 cm) seam allowance unless otherwise noted.

1. Fuse interfacing to wrong side of two bag pieces.

2. With right sides together, pin one bag piece to the other. Sew around three sides (fig. 6-13).

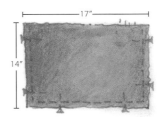

fig. 6-13

3. Make lining, the same as bag in Step 2, except use ⅝" (1.75 cm) seam allowance.

4. Make box corners on bag and lining. Fold each corner so that side and bottom seams match; this will make a point at end of bottom seam. Sew across end; trim off point (fig. 6-14). The lining seam should be 5½" (13.75 cm); the bag seam should be 6" (15 cm).

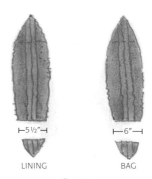

LINING   BAG

fig. 6-14

5. Turn bag right side out. On bag only, topstitch corner edges from box corner to top edge (fig. 6-15).

6. Fold top edge of bag ½″ (1.25 cm) toward wrong side. Press. Repeat for lining (fig. 6-16).

7. Center 2″ (5 cm) strip of Velcro on front of bag, 1″ (2.5 cm) down from top folded edge (fig. 6-17).

8. Fuse interfacing to wrong side of strap. Fold over one long edge ¾″ (2 cm). Double-fold other edge ⅜″ (1 cm), then ⅝″ (1.75 cm). Strap will be approximately 1″ (2.5 cm) wide. Press (fig. 6-18).

9. To make a pointed end, fold over end ¼″ (0.75 cm), then fold edges at 45° angle toward middle so that center point is in 1″ (2.5 cm) section (fig. 6-19). Note that point will be off-center.

10. On inside of strap, zigzag stitch through all layers along centerfold.

11. Center handle ends on side seam of bag, 4″ (10 cm) down from top folded edge. Topstitch as shown to hold (fig. 6-20).

fig. 6-15

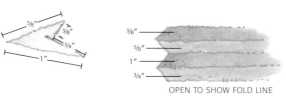

OPEN TO SHOW FOLD LINE

fig. 6-18

BAG

LINING

fig. 6-16

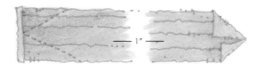

fig. 6-19

fig. 6-17

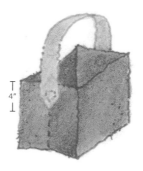

fig. 6-20

12. Pin lining inside bag, wrong sides together. Topstitch along top edges to join. Lining should be a scant ⅛″ (0.5 cm) from top (fig. 6-21).

13. Stack lining and flap fabrics. Curve two corners (fig. 6-22).

14. Center Velcro on right side of lining, 1″ (2.5 cm) from curved raw edge (fig. 6-23).

15. Prepare teddy bear appliqué and fuse to outside of flap. Using machine buttonhole stitch, stitch around all edges. Embroider eyes, nose, and mouth with hand or machine stitches.

16. Pin lining on flap, right sides together. Stitch around outside edges, leaving an opening on bottom edge for turning.

17. Clip curves and corners; turn flap right side out. Press. Topstitch ¼″ (0.75 cm) from curved edge.

18. Center flap on back of tote, ¾″ (2 cm) from top edge. Stitch a rectangle through all layers, as shown (fig. 6-24). This topstitching will close the opening used for turning.

fig. 6-21

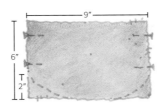

fig. 6-22

fig. 6-23

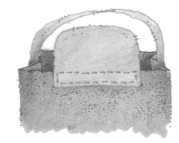

fig. 6-24

traveling teddy, a velveteen bear

* *

This soft velveteen bear will be a cherished traveling companion for your toddler. Long trips are easier when there's a special stuffed toy to hold. Finished bear is 10″ (25 cm) tall.

Supplies

Fabric	Piece	Amount	Size
Cotton velveteen	bear	½ yd (0.5 m)	See pattern
No. 5 pearl cotton			
Stuffing			
⅜″ (1 cm) satin ribbon	bow	½ yd (0.5 m)	
Heavy-duty thread			

fig. 6-25

instructions

Use ¼″ (0.75 cm) seam allowance unless otherwise noted. Use shortened stitch length and stitch each seam twice. Patterns are provided, beginning on page 127.

1. With right sides together, pin one bear front to the other. Sew center front seam (fig. 6-25).

2. Pin bear front to bear back, right sides together. Sew around outside edges, leaving a 3½″ (8.75 cm) opening on one side for turning and stuffing (fig. 6-26).

3. Clip curves. Turn bear right side out.

4. Lightly stuff ears. Sew across ears (fig. 6-27).

5. Stuff head firmly.

•tip•

Make a sleeping bag or a vest for Traveling Teddy, using leftover fabric from the Teddy Bear Quilt.

6. Stuff arms. Sew across arm/shoulder. Stuff legs; stitch line across top of leg to make joint (fig. 6-28).

7. Stuff rest of body (fig. 6-29).

8. Using quadrupled thread (page 126), close side opening with ladder stitch.

9. Embroider eyes, nose, and mouth with hand stitches as shown (fig. 6-30).

10. Tie bow around neck.

•tip•

To prevent narrow seams from raveling, use fray-checking liquid along outside edge of seam allowance, being careful not to get liquid inside seamline. Let dry.

fig. 6-26

fig. 6-27

fig. 6-28

fig. 6-29

fig. 6-30

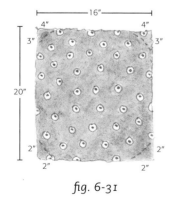

•tip•

Measure distance around top and bottom of car seat before purchasing and cutting webbed strapping.

car organizer

Strap this organizer on the back of the front seat so that crayons, coloring books, games, and other travel essentials are handy. See-through vinyl pockets let Mother keep track of the treasures that are being stashed away. Finished size is 16" × 20" (40 cm × 50 cm).

Supplies

Fabric	Piece	Amount	Cut	Size
Corduroy	Front and back	¾ yd (0.75 cm)	2	Each, 16" × 20" (40 cm × 50 cm)
Fusible heavyweight interfacing		1 yd (1 m)	2	Each, 15½" × 19½" (38.75 cm × 48.75 cm)
1" (2.5 cm) D-rings	4			
1"- (2.5 cm-) wide webbed strapping	D-ring loops	2 yd (1.9 m)	2	Each, 3½" (8.75 cm) long
	Top strap		1	22" (55 cm) long
	Bottom strap		1	44" (110 cm) long
Extra-wide double-faced bias tape		4½ yd (4.2 m)		
See-through vinyl	Top pocket	½ yd (0.5 m)	1	4½" × 14" (11.25 cm × 35 cm)
	Middle pocket		1	3½" × 16" (8.75 cm × 40 cm)
	Bottom pocket		1	4½" × 16" (11.25 cm × 40 cm)

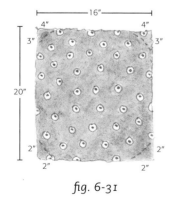

fig. 6-31

instructions

Use ½" (1.25 cm) seam allowance unless otherwise noted.

1. Fuse interfacing to wrong side of organizer front. Repeat for organizer back.

2. Pin organizer front to organizer back, wrong sides together. Shape top and bottom corners as shown (fig. 6-31).

3. Trim bottom pocket to match bottom curve on organizer.

4. Pin purchased binding to all edges of top pocket; top and bottom edges of middle pocket; and top edge of bottom pocket. Topstitch in place (fig. 6-32).

5. Position pockets on front of organizer and pin in place. Trim top corners to accommodate curve if necessary (fig. 6-33).

6. Divide pockets into compartments by stitching through all layers (fig. 6-34).

7. Treat cut ends of straps with fray-check liquid to prevent raveling.

8. Insert each 3½″ (8.75 cm) strap through two D-rings. Make a loop, position and stitch in place on organizer back, inside the seam allowance. Position top and bottom straps, then stitch in place inside seam allowance (fig. 6-35).

9. With wrong sides together, pin organizer front to organizer back. Cover outside edges with purchased bias binding. Pin in place; topstitch through all layers from front (fig. 6-36).

10. Fold top straps toward top edge. Stitch through all layers. (fig. 6-37).

•tip•

When stitching on vinyl, use a longer stitch length. Short stitches will cause vinyl to tear along seamline. A roller foot or Teflon foot may be helpful.

•tip•

Purchased bias is usually folded so that one side is slightly wider than the other. The wider side should go on the back; the narrower side goes on the front.

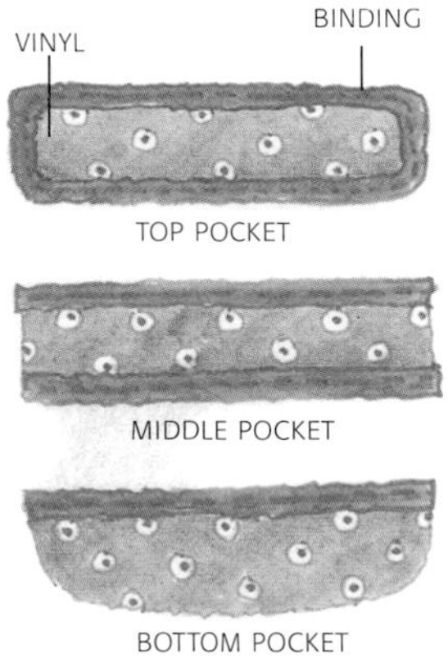

VINYL BINDING

TOP POCKET

MIDDLE POCKET

BOTTOM POCKET

fig. 6-32

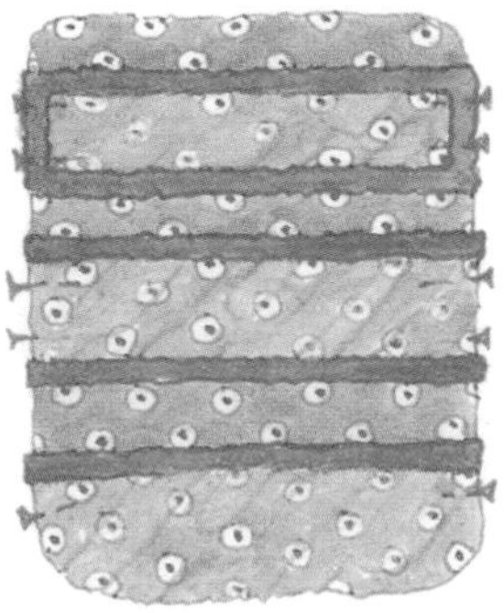

fig. 6-33

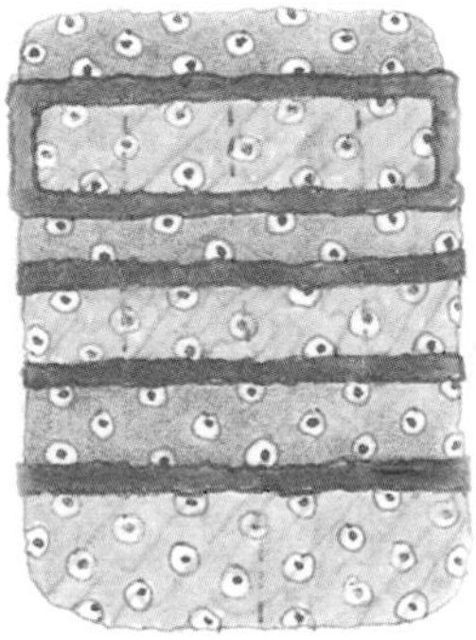

fig. 6-34

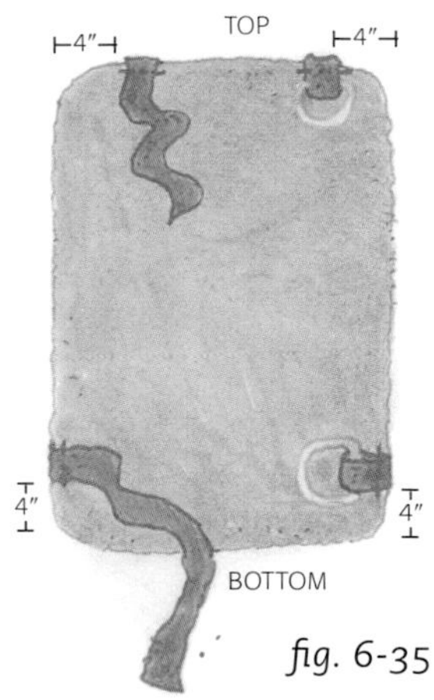

├4″┤ TOP ├4″┤

BOTTOM

fig. 6-35

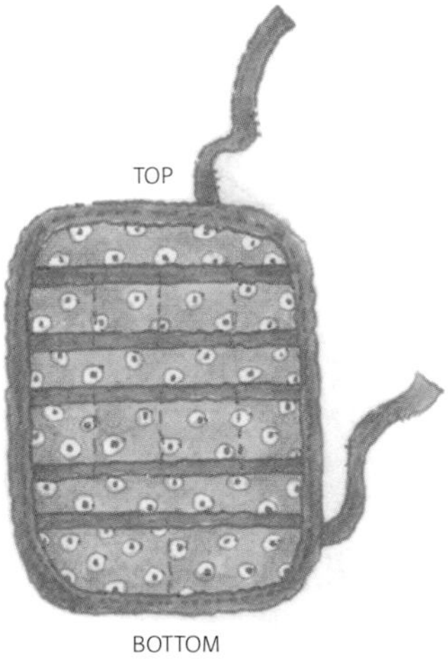

TOP

BOTTOM

fig. 6-36

BACK

fig. 6-37

Hints and Techniques 7

Appliqués

Preparing Appliqués

Trace designs, using a light table or a windowpane on a sunny day. Turn designs into iron-on appliqués by using paper-backed fusible adhesive.

Method 1: trace pattern on back

1. Trace appliqué design onto paper backing of fusible adhesive. Take care to reverse letters or other designs that have a definite direction (fig. 7-1).

2. Fuse adhesive to wrong side of appliqué fabric (fig. 7-2). Cut out design.

3. Peel away paper backing. For easy removal of the paper backing, score it (make an X) with a straight pin.

4. Position appliqué, adhesive side down, on right side of base fabric. Follow manufacturer's directions to fuse in place with iron (fig. 7-3).

5. Sew around appliqué with machine stitch to hold edges in place. Use straight stitch, satin stitch, blanket stitch, or other decorative stitch as desired (fig. 7-4).

sewing order for appliqués

When there are several appliqué layers, work from background to foreground. Start stitching around background, or underlapping, sections. Stitch around foreground, or overlapping, sections last.

fig. 7-1

fig. 7-2

fig. 7-3

fig. 7-4

115

fig. 7-5

stitching details

Take time for the details, for these add life to an appliquéd piece. On the Castle Quilt (page 3), the details—bricks, roof lines, vines, flowers, leaves—are stitched with rayon machine embroidery threads in free-motion technique (see page 117).

Draw stitching lines with chalk, light-soluble ink, or other erasable marker. Then free-motion stitch over each line at least three times. Remember to place a tear-away stabilizer under the fabric to prevent fabric distortion, then remove it when the stitching is completed.

Method 2: pin pattern to front

1. Fuse adhesive to wrong side of appliqué fabric.

2. Pin pattern to right side of fabric and cut out (fig. 7-5).

3. Continue as in Method 1, Steps 3–5.

Stitching Appliqués

Once appliqués have been fused in position, edges must be stitched down. Use machine straight stitch, blanket stitch, or satin stitch (see page 123). Threads can match or contrast. Use a stabilizer (see page 125) under the fabric while stitching, then remove it when finished. A stabilizer will also prevent satin stitches or blanket stitches from tunneling.

The Castle Quilt (page 3) and Pillow Sham (page 8) feature free-motion stitching around the edges of each appliqué. Be sure to go over each line at least three times. The repeated lines blend together visually and add a hand-drawn look to the finished piece. With practice, your stitching lines will be practically identical, one over the other.

If you want a definite outline around each appliqué, use a contrasting thread color and machine buttonhole stitch.

Bias Binding

Detailed instructions are given for each project, but the general procedure is as follows:

1. Trim all quilt edges with a rotary cutter and ruler, making sure the sides are even and square.

2. Pin the bias binding to the front of the quilt, right sides together and edges matching. Pin carefully about every 4″ (10 cm). Work on a flat surface so you don't accidentally pin in any wrinkles.

3. Sew through all layers to hold the binding in place.

4. Fold the binding to the back of the quilt, covering the raw edges. Slip-stitch the binding in place along the back.

An alternate method is to sew binding to the back, fold it over the raw edge to the front, then topstitch in place by machine on the front.

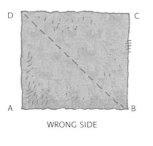

WRONG SIDE

fig. 7-6

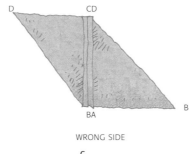

WRONG SIDE

fig. 7-7

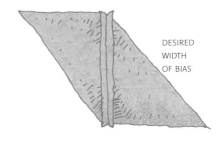

DESIRED WIDTH OF BIAS

fig. 7-8

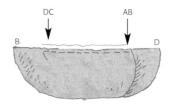

fig. 7-9

Continuous Bias Binding

1. Start with a square of fabric A 36″ (90 cm) square will make more than 16 yards (14.8 meters) of 2″ (5 cm) wide bias.

2. Cut diagonally from corner to corner (on bias) (fig. 7-6).

3. Pin the two halves right sides together, matching the raw edges along the straight grain. Stitch, using a ¼″ (0.75 cm) seam allowance. Press the seam open (fig. 7-7).

4. Mark the width of the bias parallel to the bias edge (fig. 7-8).

5. With right sides together, match the bottom edge (BAB) to the top edge (DCD), offsetting by the desired width of the bias (fig. 7-9). Stitch, then press the seam open.

6. Starting at the marked end, cut the bias strip, measuring as you go (fig. 7-10).

7. Using a bias pressing device, pull the bias through the device and press the edges toward the middle (fig. 7-11).

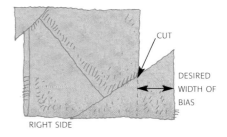

RIGHT SIDE

CUT

DESIRED WIDTH OF BIAS

fig. 7-10

Free-Motion Sewing

Free-motion sewing means sewing with the feed dogs down so that you can move the fabric freely under the needle in any direction you choose. Free-motion techniques are useful for both embroidery and machine quilting.

1. Place your fabric in a hoop. Place outer hoop on a table, put fabric on top, then press down with the inner hoop. Pull fabric to straighten and use screw to adjust tension.

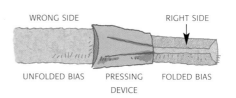

WRONG SIDE · RIGHT SIDE

UNFOLDED BIAS · PRESSING DEVICE · FOLDED BIAS

fig. 7-11

2. Lower the feed dogs on your machine.

3. Use a darning foot. It moves up and down while sewing, pressing down on the fabric only when the stitch is being made.

4. Use normal tension settings; set stitch width and stitch length to 0. Sew with "needle down" setting. You can also do free-motion work with a zigzag stitch.

5. Take one stitch; pull bobbin thread through fabric to top. Hold threads and take 3–4 more stitches in place to lock thread. Clip thread ends and continue sewing.

6. To practice free-motion sewing, write your name, make loops, circles, boxes, and other shapes. Start and end each design with a lockstitch (stitch in place 3–4 times). To stitch a separate design that is close to, but not connected to, the first design, raise foot lever, move fabric to next starting point, lower tension bar, and start sewing. Clip thread tails later.

7. The machine has to be stitching faster than the fabric is moving. For best results, run the machine at a medium to fast speed, then move the hoop smoothly. Fast, abrupt movements will break the needle; very slow movement can cause build-up of bobbin thread.

Interfacing

Fusible interfacings are very useful. Simply follow manufacturer's directions and fuse to the wrong side of the fabric. Once interfaced, the fabric becomes stiffer, giving an item like a collar a crisper look.

Fusible interfacings are available in a variety of weights, from light to heavy. The item being sewn and the fabric itself help to determine the best weight to choose. For example, a lightweight interfacing is fine for the Dragon Hood (page 78), but a heavyweight interfacing should be used in the Backpack (page 48).

Interfacing is also useful when working with fabrics that ravel easily or are slippery to handle. Typical costume fabrics like lamés and polyester silks are easier to work with when interfaced first. For example, try fusible tricot interfacing on lamé fabrics.

Fusible interfacing is commonly available in 20" (50 cm) widths. If fabric is wider, fuse additional strips of interfacing to fabric as needed.

Here are two ways to use fusible interfacing.

1. Using pattern, cut fabric and interfacing separately. Trim seam allowance off interfacing. Center on wrong side of fabric and fuse. The

advantage of this method is that there will be no interfacing in the seam allowance.

2. Fuse interfacing to wrong side of fabric, then cut out pattern. This method is easy, but there will be interfacing in the seam allowance, making it bulkier.

fig. 7-12

Ladder Stitch

Use this stitch to close seam openings (fig. 7-12).

Lettuce Edging

Use this edging technique to hem sheer fabrics, such as chiffon. This edging is used on the Fairy costumes (page 92).

Set machine to short stitch length and narrow zigzag, so that left swing of needle is in fabric and right swing is just off the fabric. The zigzag stitch will roll and whip the edge of the fabric while sewing. To ruffle the edge, gently stretch the fabric in front of needle only during stitching process. This technique works best on a bias edge.

Machine Quilting

For machine quilting, use a machine stitch length of 8–10 stitches per inch (3–4 stitches per cm). Sew from the center toward the edges. Roll the side and bottom edges toward the center. Stitch by machine from the center toward the bottom edge, unrolling as you sew. Then turn the quilt 180° and repeat the process, again sewing from the center toward the top edge. Repeat, rerolling and refolding as needed. An even-feed foot will minimize puckering, though you will still need to keep an eye on your fabric and smooth it as necessary as it feeds under the needle.

You can also quilt by machine using the *free-motion method*. Drop the feed dogs, and use a special quilting foot and needle designed for machine quilting. While sewing, use your hands to move the fabric under the needle. The Castle Quilt uses stippling, spirals, and echo outlines (page 3). There are several machine feet recommended for free-motion quilting; use whatever works best on your machine.

Use machine quilting threads that match the bottom and top layers of your quilt. Monofilament thread will also work. You may want to choose contrasting threads for quilting emphasis.

•tip•

When working on large pieces, such as a quilt, put your sewing machine on a good-sized table, then use the table extension for your free-arm machine. The table holds the quilt while you're working on it, so the weight is not on your lap or pulling against the needle.

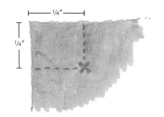

fig. 7-13

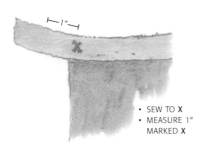

- SEW TO **X**
- MEASURE 1"
  MARKED **X**

fig. 7-14

- PLACE **X** ON **Y**
- CONTINUE
  SEWING

fig. 7-15

QUILT FRONT

fig. 7-16

Mitered Corners

Here is an easy way to make a mitered corner when attaching bias binding to a quilt.

1. Starting in the middle of the bottom edge of the quilt, place binding on the front of the quilt, right sides together and edges matching.

2. Stitch, stopping several inches away from the corner. Mark ¼″ (0.75 cm) from each corner with a pin (fig. 7-13).

3. Sew to the first pin; lock stitch. Measure 1″ (2.5 cm) of binding; mark with a pin (fig. 7-14).

4. Match the pin on the binding to the second corner pin. Lock stitch, then continue sewing (fig. 7-15).

5. When the bias binding is turned over to the back, the corner fold will be mitered (fig. 7-16).

Pressing

One of the secrets of a great-looking finished project is to turn on your iron—and use it often. It's the heat and steam that does the work, so it's unnecessary to push down on your iron. When you push down and drag the iron across the fabric, you're likely to stretch it. It's better to press, then lift and move the iron.

Press as you go. For example, sew a seam, then press the seam. Fold an edge, then press the fold. Press a hem, then stitch the hem.

Always use a pressing cloth when ironing fabrics like these: vinyl-covered fabric; lamés; sheers, such as organza, chiffon, and tulle; synthetic fabrics, such as taffeta, satin, lamé, and polyester silk. Most polyester fabrics press well.

Quilts, How to Make

1. *Prepare fabric.* Toddlers drag their possessions everywhere, so frequent washings are to be expected. Before you sew, preshrink fabric by washing and drying on hottest settings recommended by manufacturer, then press with a steam iron. Washing also removes excess sizing and dyes that might irritate sensitive skin.

2. *Piece quilt top.* In this book, several methods are used. For the Courthouse Steps Quilt (page 25), strips are sewn around a center square.

For Teddy Bear Quilt (page 103), rectangles are sewn together to make blocks. For the Castle Quilt (page 3), motifs are appliquéd.

3. *Add borders.* Add borders to sides of quilt first, then add to top and bottom edges.

4. *Piece backing.* Although there are fabrics available in 90″ (225 cm) widths, many stitchers prefer backing their quilts with coordinating fabrics. If fabrics are narrower than the quilt top, you'll have to do some minimal piecing. Fabrics on the back should have the same fiber content as on front; that is, a pieced cotton top should have a cotton backing.

5. *Assemble layers.* Square up quilt top using rotary cutter and ruler. Cut backing and batting bigger than quilt top—approximately 3″–4″ (7.5–10 cm) extra all around. Anchor the backing, wrong side up, to a flat surface with masking tape, smoothing the backing without stretching it. Center the batting on top of the backing fabric, then center the pieced quilt top, right side up, as the top layer.

6. *Baste layers together.* Starting in center and working toward edges, pin with rustproof brass quilting pins every 3″–4″ (7.5–10 cm) in a grid pattern, taking care to avoid excessive puckering in backing. Try to avoid pinning along quilting lines. Layers are now ready to be sewn together, or quilted.

7. *Quilt through all layers.* Quilt, using hand or machine stitches. Start in the center and work toward the edges. Projects in this book are quilted by machine (see also Machine Quilting, page 119).

8. *Bind quilt edges.* Square up and trim quilt, using a ruler and rotary cutter. Using your machine, sew binding to front of quilt. Trim away half the seam allowance. Fold binding to back, covering edges of quilt. Catch folded binding edge on back side of quilt with invisible hand stitches (see also Mitered Corners, page 120.)

9. *Date and sign quilt.* Make a label for back, then embroider by hand or machine, or write using permanent ink. Test on scrap first to make sure you can see thread or ink color.

Ruffles

• •

Beautiful ruffles are evenly gathered and hang straight. Follow these steps to make a perfect gathered ruffle:

•tip•

To make your own pressing cloth, cut a piece of muslin 18″ × 24″ (45 cm × 60 cm). Overcast raw edges with a serger or machine overcast stitch.

•tip•

Square up individual quilt blocks with ruler and rotary cutter before joining together. Square up pieced top again before adding borders.

•option•

There are quilt-basting adhesive sprays now available. Read labels carefully to determine if these products are water soluble and if sewing will be affected. It's always a good idea to make (and wash) a few test samples to be sure. If allergies or fabric flammability are a concern, check with the manufacturer before using.

1. Cut ruffle length 2–3 times longer than base fabric length. Join all ends; if wrong side of fabric ruffle will be exposed, use French seams to join. Hem bottom edge.

2. Starting ¼" (0.75 cm) from top edge and using the longest machine stitch length, sew two rows of gathering stitches along the top edge of ruffle. Each row should be ¼" (0.75 cm) apart.

   For a long ruffle, divide ruffle fabric strip into two to four sections, then sew a separate set of gathering threads in each section. By gathering shorter sections, threads will be less likely to break when pulled up for gathering.

3. Mark quarter-points on ruffle and base fabric.

4. Lay base fabric on table or other flat surface, right side up. Place ruffle on top, right side down, matching raw edges.

5. Pin ruffle to base fabric at marked points.

6. Pull gathering threads to form ruffle.

7. Distribute gathers evenly. Allow extra fullness at corners.

8. Holding raw edges, give ruffle a firm tug to make gathers line up perpendicular to ruffle.

9. Pin carefully, about every ½" (1.25 cm).

10. Stitch close to the second line of stitching. To stitch around corners, sew three stitches diagonally across corner point.

11. Topstitch from right side to secure seam allowance.

Most books, this one included, tell you to use two gathering threads (Step 2). However, if you want to make a perfect ruffle, use three gathering threads. When attaching the ruffle, sew along the middle thread. Yes, you'll have to remove the bottom thread after the ruffle is attached.

Satin Stitch

Machine satin stitch is an easy way to finish the edges of your appliqués. It gives a smooth and professional look to your project. Here are some recommendations to make your satin stitch look good.

Supplies

Needles

Use size 80/12 embroidery sewing machine needles. If you're using metallic, rayon, or other specialty threads, use a needle designed to handle those threads. Be sure to start every new project with a brand new needle.

Threads

Use 30-wt or 40-wt machine embroidery threads in the needle. Cotton, rayon, acrylic, metallic, silk, and polyester threads are available. Use lightweight machine-embroidery bobbin. (Higher numbers mean finer and lighter machine threads.)

Stabilizer

Stabilizer is required between the fabric and feed dogs in order to make a good satin stitch. Otherwise, the fabric will distort and tunnel.

Try a *nonwoven stabilizer* that can be torn away from the threads after the appliqué is sewn. Just be careful not to rip out the stitches while removing the stabilizer.

Machine feet and settings

Use an *open-toed appliqué foot*. It has a groove on the bottom of the foot to ride over the satin stitches. The open toe makes it easy for you to see where you're sewing.

Shorten *stitch length*. The zigzag stitches should lie next to each other, covering the fabric underneath without piling up. If your machine has a preset stitch length, you may have to adjust it, depending on the threads you're using.

Start with a medium *stitch width*, then adjust as desired. When sewn, most of the zigzag stitch should be on the appliqué fabric. The right swing of the zigzag should put the needle just over the edge of the appliqué into the base fabric. You can vary the stitch width while you are sewing by turning the knob or tapping the stitch width button.

The *tension* for the top thread may be slightly looser than for regular sewing. The top threads should be pulled to the underneath side of the fabric. Bobbin thread should not be visible on top of fabric. Match bobbin thread color to top thread to eliminate problem of bobbin thread "bleeding" to top. Many newer machines have automatic tension settings.

fig. 7-17

fig. 7-18

fig. 7-19

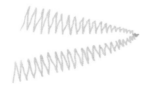

fig. 7-20

If the tension is too tight, override the automatic setting and reduce the tension in small increments until you find the best setting. Record this setting in your notebook.

If your machine has an adjustable *pressure setting* for the presser foot, use the lightest setting. This may enable you to move the fabric without stopping while sewing satin stitch around soft curves. Be sure to practice on some scraps first to see if this technique will work for you.

Choose the *needle-down position* while sewing. This allows you to pivot the fabric accurately.

Sewing Techniques for Satin Stitch

Start and end in the middle of a straight line. Do not start at a corner or a point.

Secure your first and last stitches with a *lockstitch*. Use a preset stitch, or stitch in place (stitch length 0) three or four times.

To *change stitch width* as you are sewing, turn the knob or tap the stitch width button while continuing to stitch. It may take some practice, but this is an important technique to master.

To *pivot* fabric, stop with the needle down. Lift the presser foot, and move the fabric as needed, then lower the presser foot and continue stitching. On sharp curves, you may need to pivot your fabric after every stitch. Remember to raise and lower the presser foot every time you stop to pivot fabric. If you forget to lower the presser foot, the tension will not be engaged.

Square corners are easy to sew. Stitch to the corner, and stop with the needle down on the outside edge of the corner (fig. 7-17). Pivot fabric 90°, then continue sewing (fig. 7-18). To sew around *curves*, pivot when the needle is on the inside of a concave curve or the outside of a convex curve (fig. 7-19). To form *points*, narrow the stitch width as you sew into the point; widen the stitch width as you sew away from the point (fig. 7-20).

Stabilizers

There are many stabilizers available, but they all serve the same purpose—to keep the fabric from shifting or distorting during the sewing process. The stabilizer is placed between the fabric and the feed dogs. A stabililzer will also prevent satin stitches or blanket stitches from tunneling.

Excess stabilizers should be removed after the sewing is completed. Nonwoven stablizers that can be easily torn or cut away from the stitches are very popular. Fusible stabilizers have a mild adhesive and can be ironed to the back of the fabric, then peeled off later. Others are water- or heat-soluble and can be dissolved with water or heat.

When removing stabilizers, take care not to pull out any stitches. Hold the stitches down with one hand and gently pull off the stabilizer with the other.

You'll have to do some practice tests to find the best stabilizer for the combination of fabric and threads that your project requires. Remember to record the results in your notebook.

Thread, Quadrupled

When attaching buttons or for extra reinforcement in seams that are sewn by hand, use quadrupled thread in the needle (fig. 7-21).

Vinyl

Vinyl is used for the pockets of the Car Organizer (page 112). When stitching on vinyl, use a longer stitch length. Short stitches will cause vinyl to tear along seamline. A roller foot or Teflon foot may be helpful. You may also use tissue paper to cover vinyl. It removes easily after stitching.

To make fabric water-resistant, as for the Rain Poncho (page 52) and other nursery school items, use iron-on vinyl. Fuse the vinyl to the right side of the fabric, then cut out the pattern pieces. Fusible vinyl is most commonly available in a narrow 17″ (42.5 cm) width.

Extra handling can cause vinyl-coated fabric to look crackled and wrinkled. To restore a smooth, finished look, iron carefully with a pressing cloth.

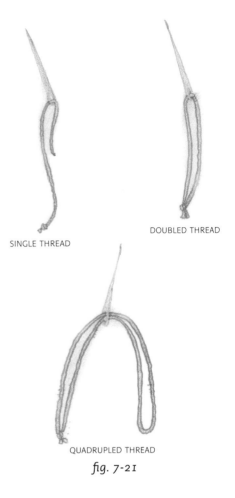

SINGLE THREAD

DOUBLED THREAD

QUADRUPLED THREAD

fig. 7-21

Patterns

Unless otherwise specified, the following patterns should be enlarged by 200 percent or redrawn on a scale of ½:1 inch. Do not enlarge shaded patterns on pages 144 and 145.

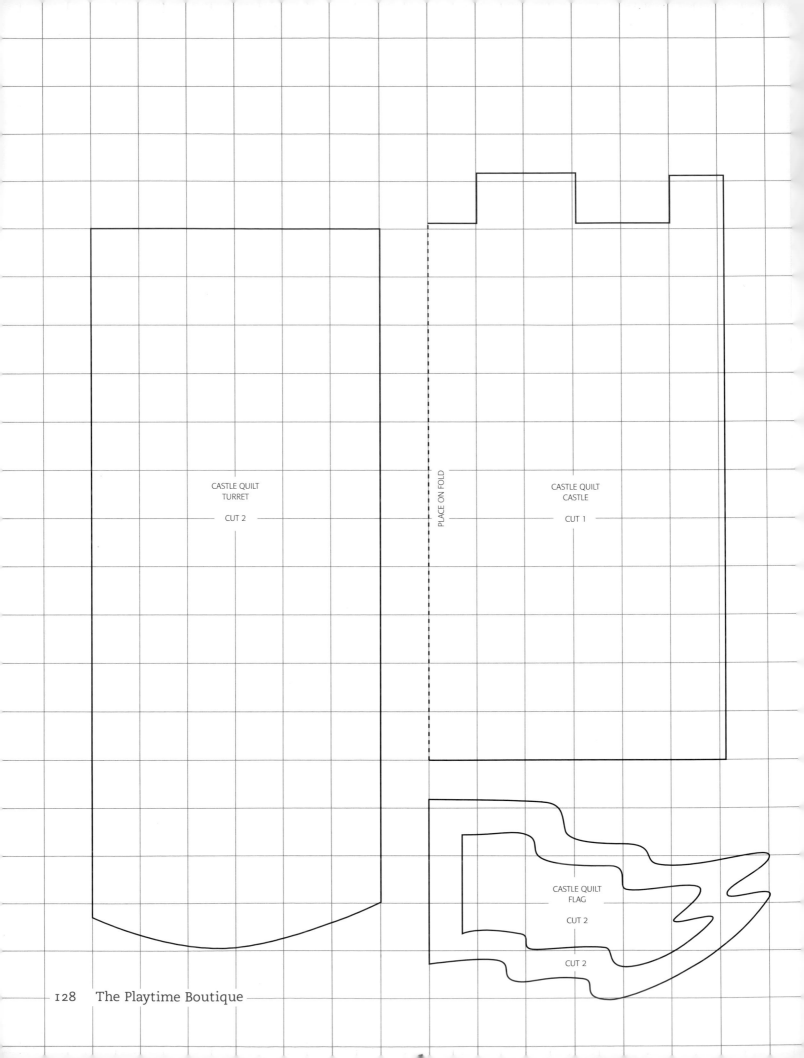

CASTLE QUILT
TURRET

CUT 2

PLACE ON FOLD

CASTLE QUILT
CASTLE

CUT 1

CASTLE QUILT
FLAG

CUT 2

CUT 2

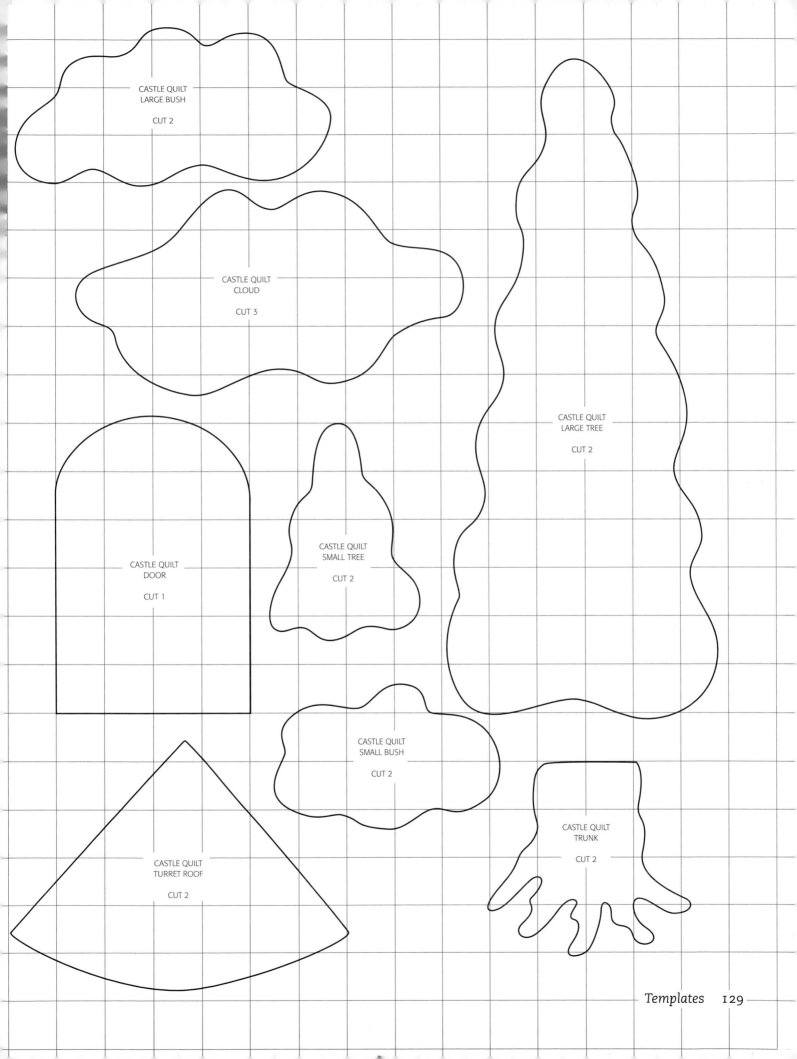

CASTLE QUILT
LARGE BUSH

CUT 2

CASTLE QUILT
CLOUD

CUT 3

CASTLE QUILT
LARGE TREE

CUT 2

CASTLE QUILT
DOOR

CUT 1

CASTLE QUILT
SMALL TREE

CUT 2

CASTLE QUILT
SMALL BUSH

CUT 2

CASTLE QUILT
TRUNK

CUT 2

CASTLE QUILT
TURRET ROOF

CUT 2

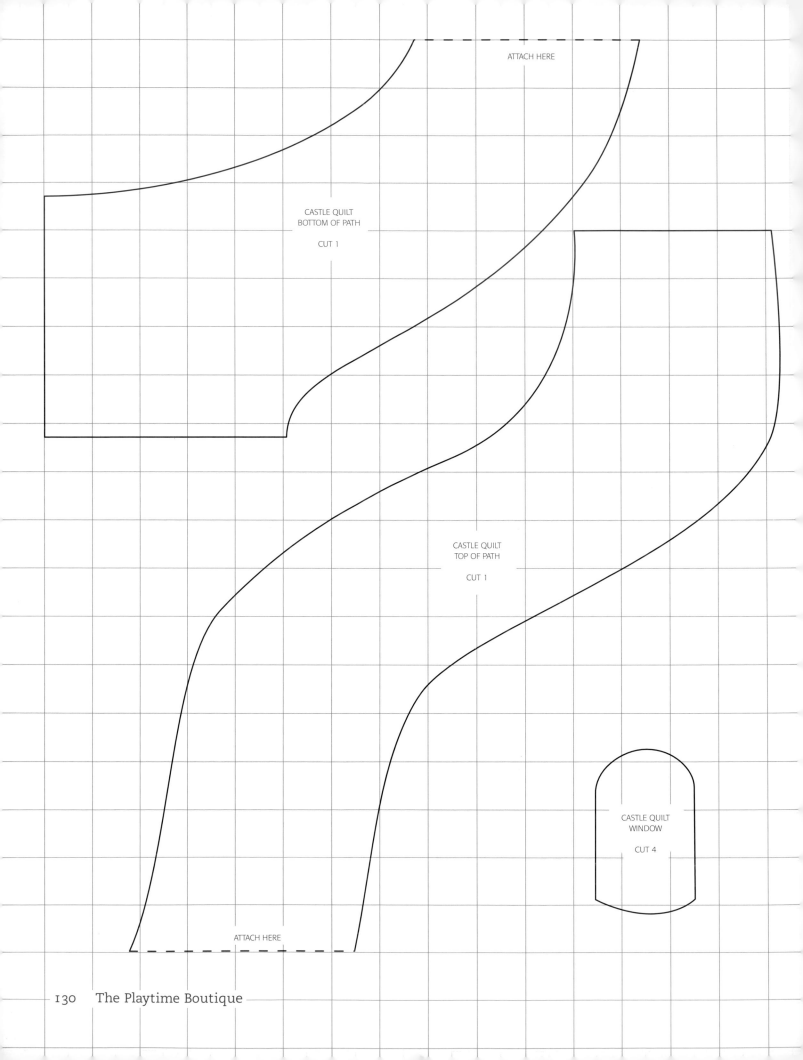

ATTACH HERE

CASTLE QUILT
BOTTOM OF PATH

CUT 1

CASTLE QUILT
TOP OF PATH

CUT 1

CASTLE QUILT
WINDOW

CUT 4

ATTACH HERE

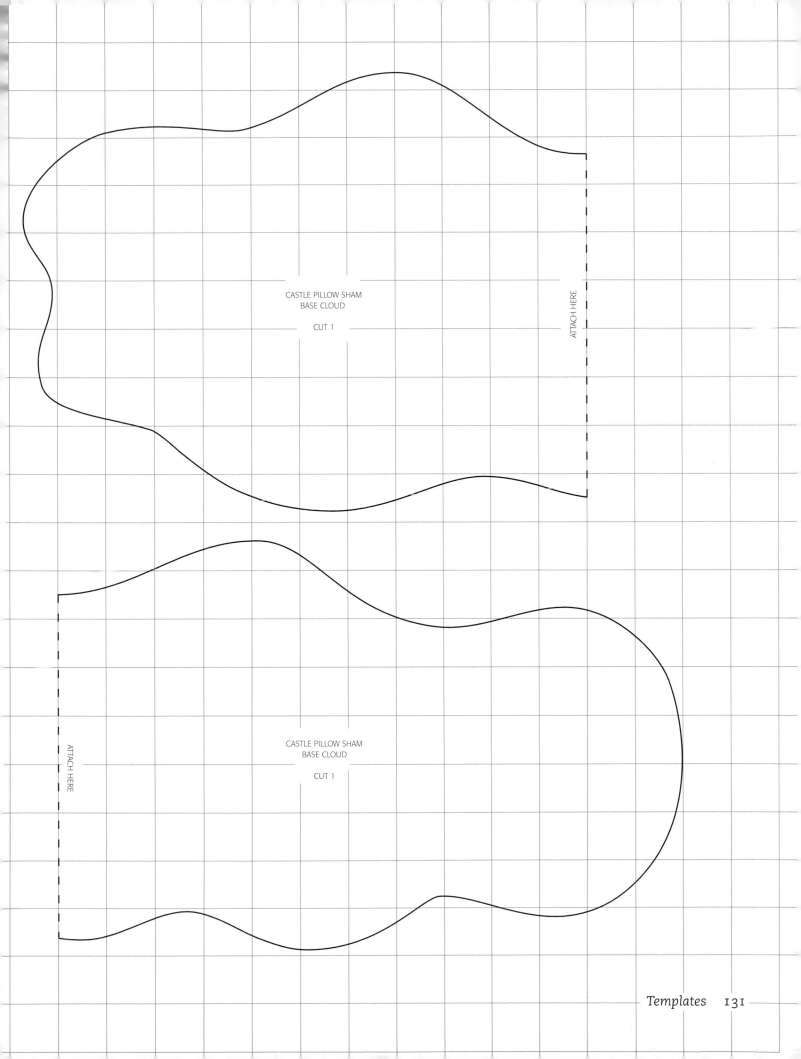

CASTLE PILLOW SHAM
BASE CLOUD

CUT 1

ATTACH HERE

ATTACH HERE

CASTLE PILLOW SHAM
BASE CLOUD

CUT 1

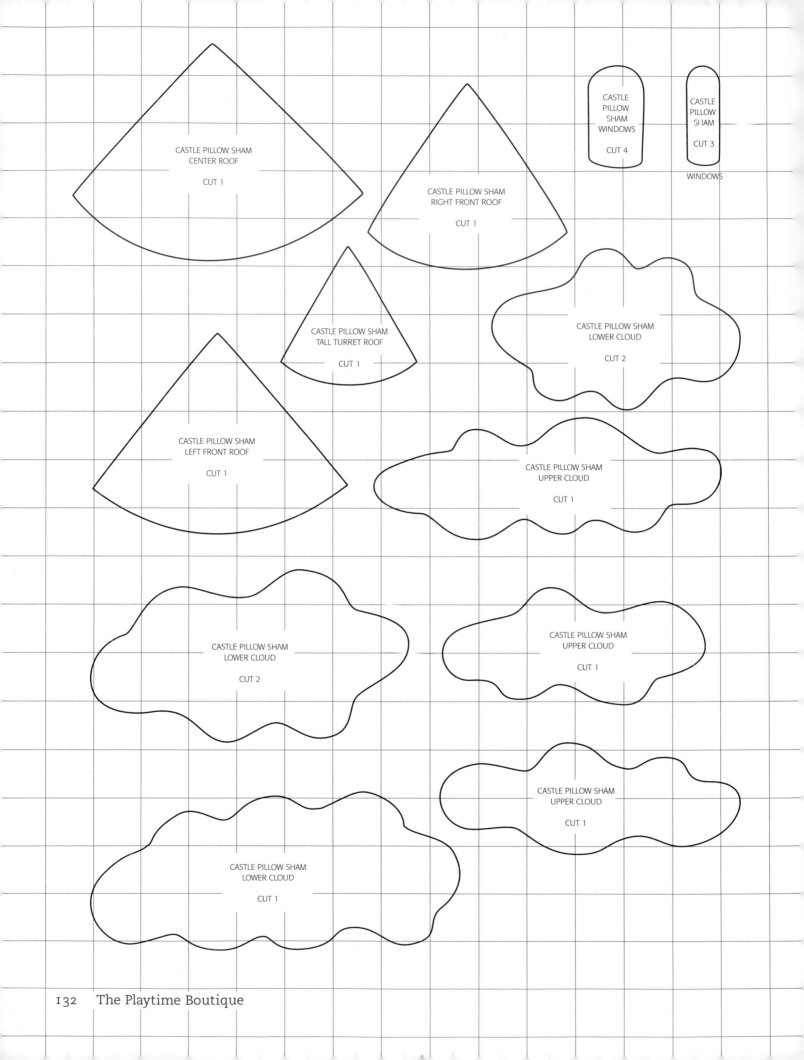

CASTLE PILLOW SHAM
CENTER ROOF

CUT 1

CASTLE PILLOW SHAM
RIGHT FRONT ROOF

CUT 1

CASTLE
PILLOW
SHAM
WINDOWS

CUT 4

CASTLE
PILLOW
SHAM

CUT 3

WINDOWS

CASTLE PILLOW SHAM
TALL TURRET ROOF

CUT 1

CASTLE PILLOW SHAM
LOWER CLOUD

CUT 2

CASTLE PILLOW SHAM
LEFT FRONT ROOF

CUT 1

CASTLE PILLOW SHAM
UPPER CLOUD

CUT 1

CASTLE PILLOW SHAM
LOWER CLOUD

CUT 2

CASTLE PILLOW SHAM
UPPER CLOUD

CUT 1

CASTLE PILLOW SHAM
UPPER CLOUD

CUT 1

CASTLE PILLOW SHAM
LOWER CLOUD

CUT 1

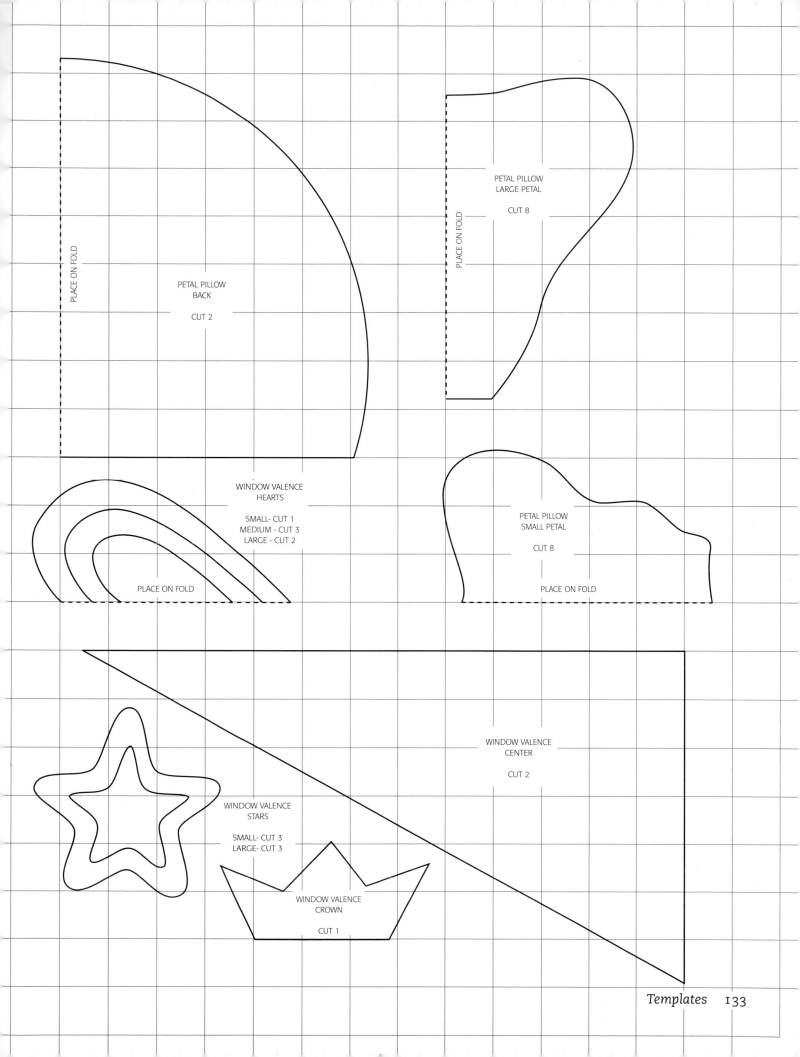

PETAL PILLOW
LARGE PETAL

CUT 8

PLACE ON FOLD

PETAL PILLOW
BACK

CUT 2

PLACE ON FOLD

WINDOW VALENCE
HEARTS

SMALL- CUT 1
MEDIUM - CUT 3
LARGE - CUT 2

PLACE ON FOLD

PETAL PILLOW
SMALL PETAL

CUT 8

PLACE ON FOLD

WINDOW VALENCE
CENTER

CUT 2

WINDOW VALENCE
STARS

SMALL- CUT 3
LARGE- CUT 3

WINDOW VALENCE
CROWN

CUT 1

Templates 133

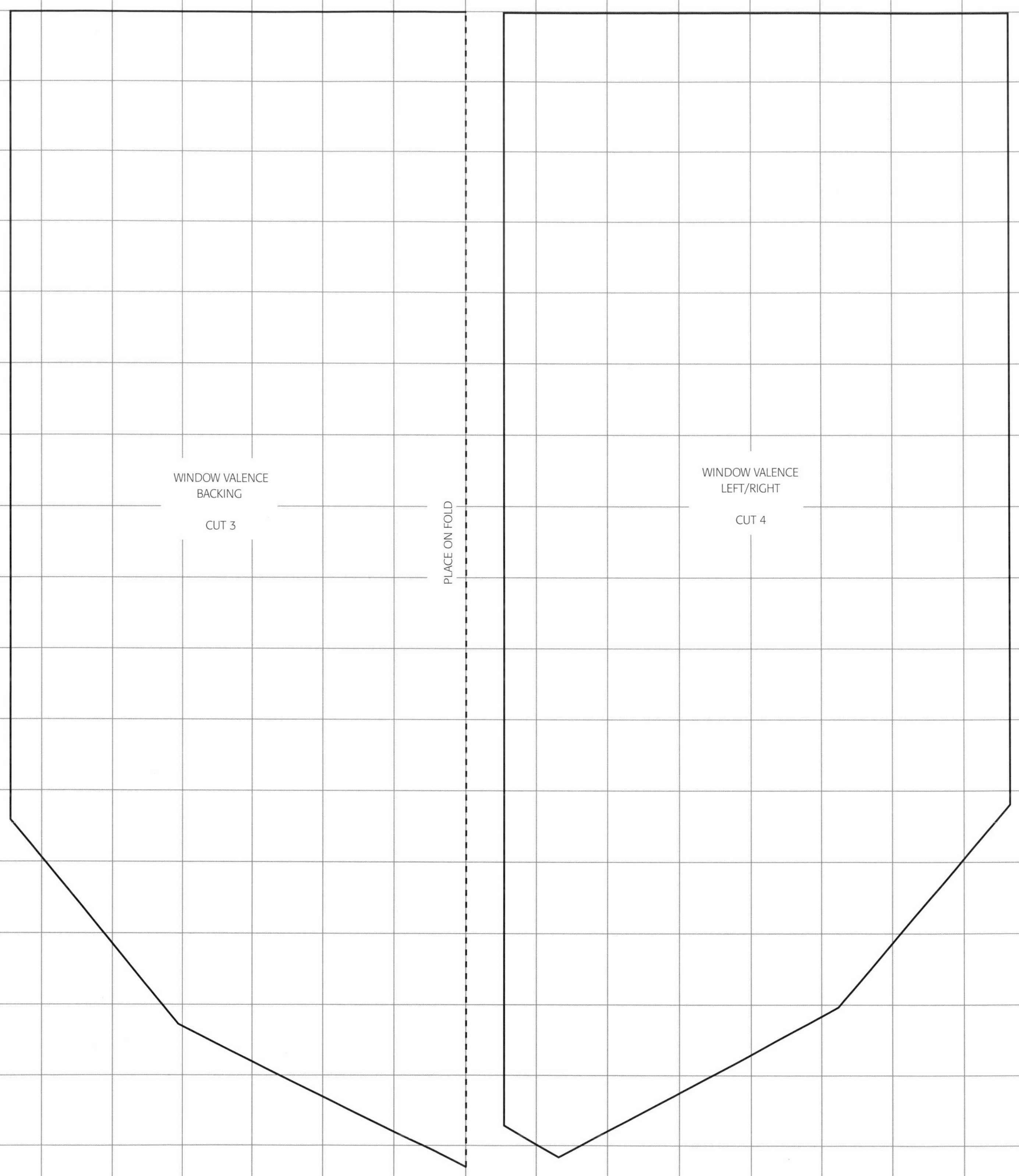

WINDOW VALENCE
BACKING

CUT 3

WINDOW VALENCE
LEFT/RIGHT

CUT 4

PLACE ON FOLD

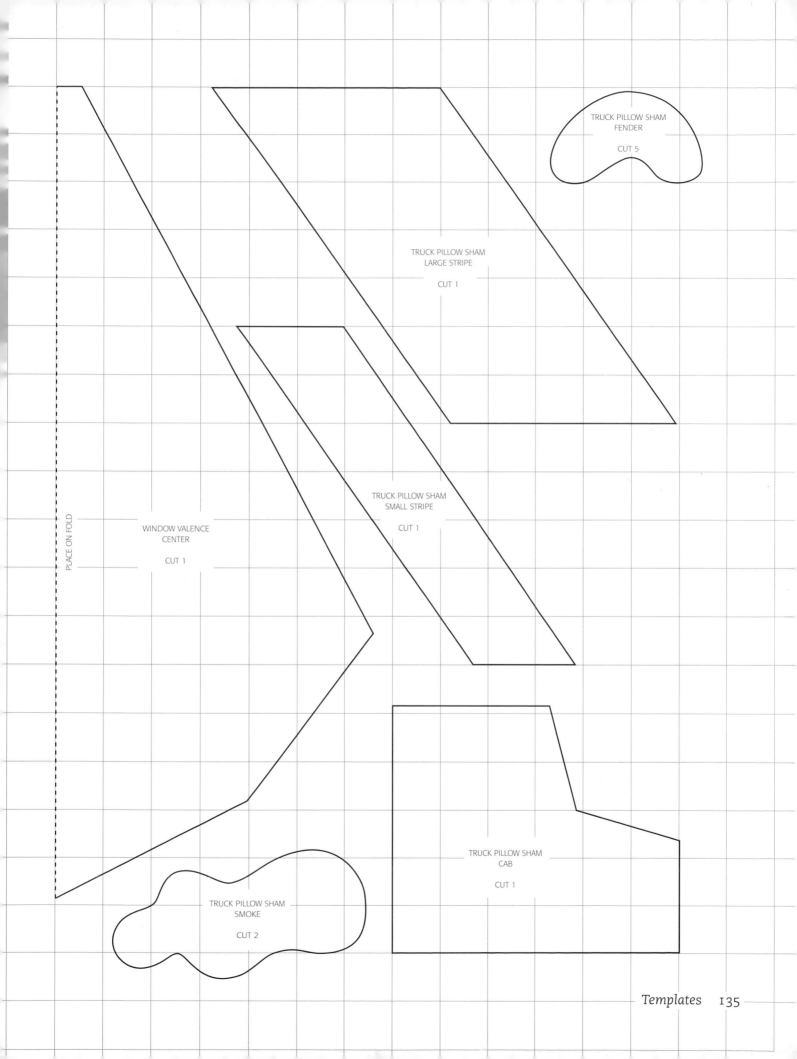

TRUCK PILLOW SHAM
FENDER

CUT 5

TRUCK PILLOW SHAM
LARGE STRIPE

CUT 1

TRUCK PILLOW SHAM
SMALL STRIPE

CUT 1

WINDOW VALENCE
CENTER

CUT 1

PLACE ON FOLD

TRUCK PILLOW SHAM
CAB

CUT 1

TRUCK PILLOW SHAM
SMOKE

CUT 2

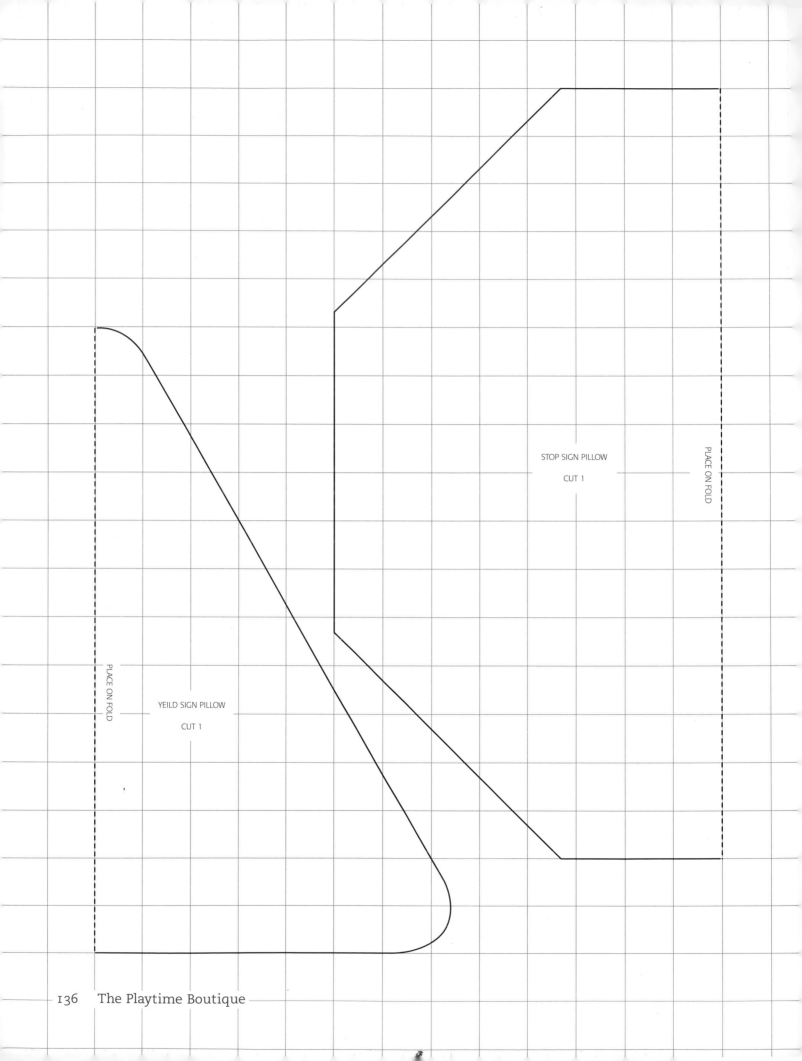

STOP SIGN PILLOW

CUT 1

PLACE ON FOLD

PLACE ON FOLD

YEILD SIGN PILLOW

CUT 1

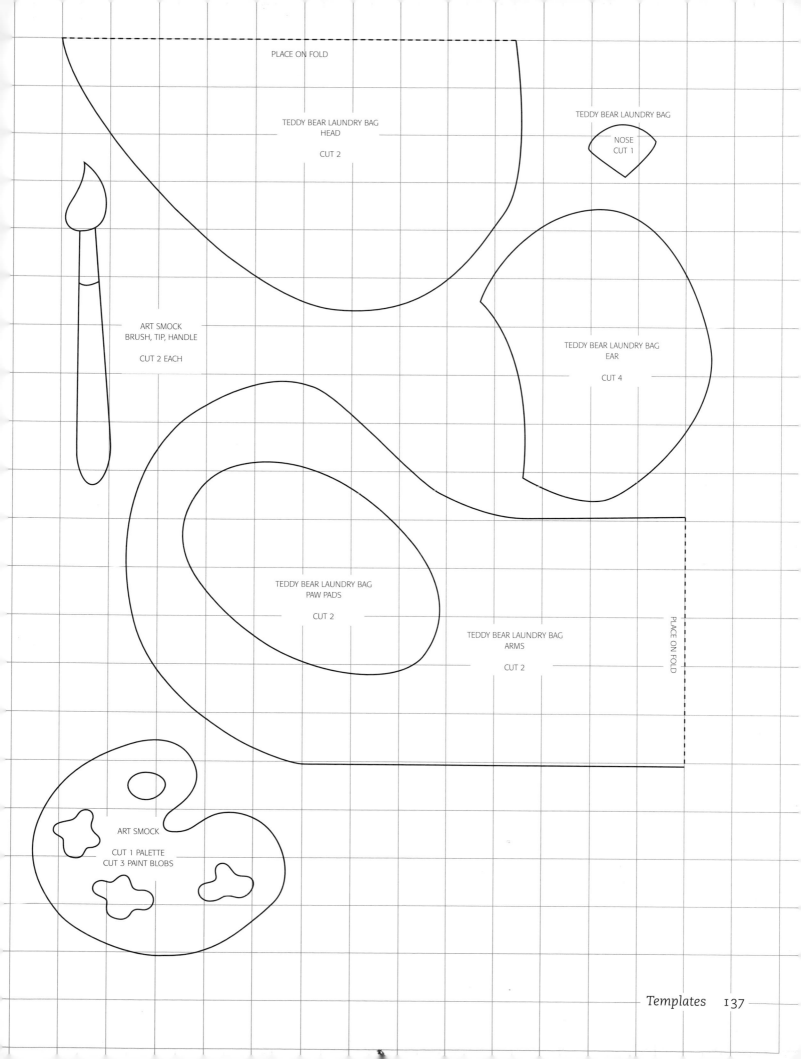

PLACE ON FOLD

TEDDY BEAR LAUNDRY BAG
HEAD

CUT 2

TEDDY BEAR LAUNDRY BAG

NOSE
CUT 1

ART SMOCK
BRUSH, TIP, HANDLE

CUT 2 EACH

TEDDY BEAR LAUNDRY BAG
EAR

CUT 4

TEDDY BEAR LAUNDRY BAG
PAW PADS

CUT 2

TEDDY BEAR LAUNDRY BAG
ARMS

CUT 2

PLACE ON FOLD

ART SMOCK

CUT 1 PALETTE
CUT 3 PAINT BLOBS

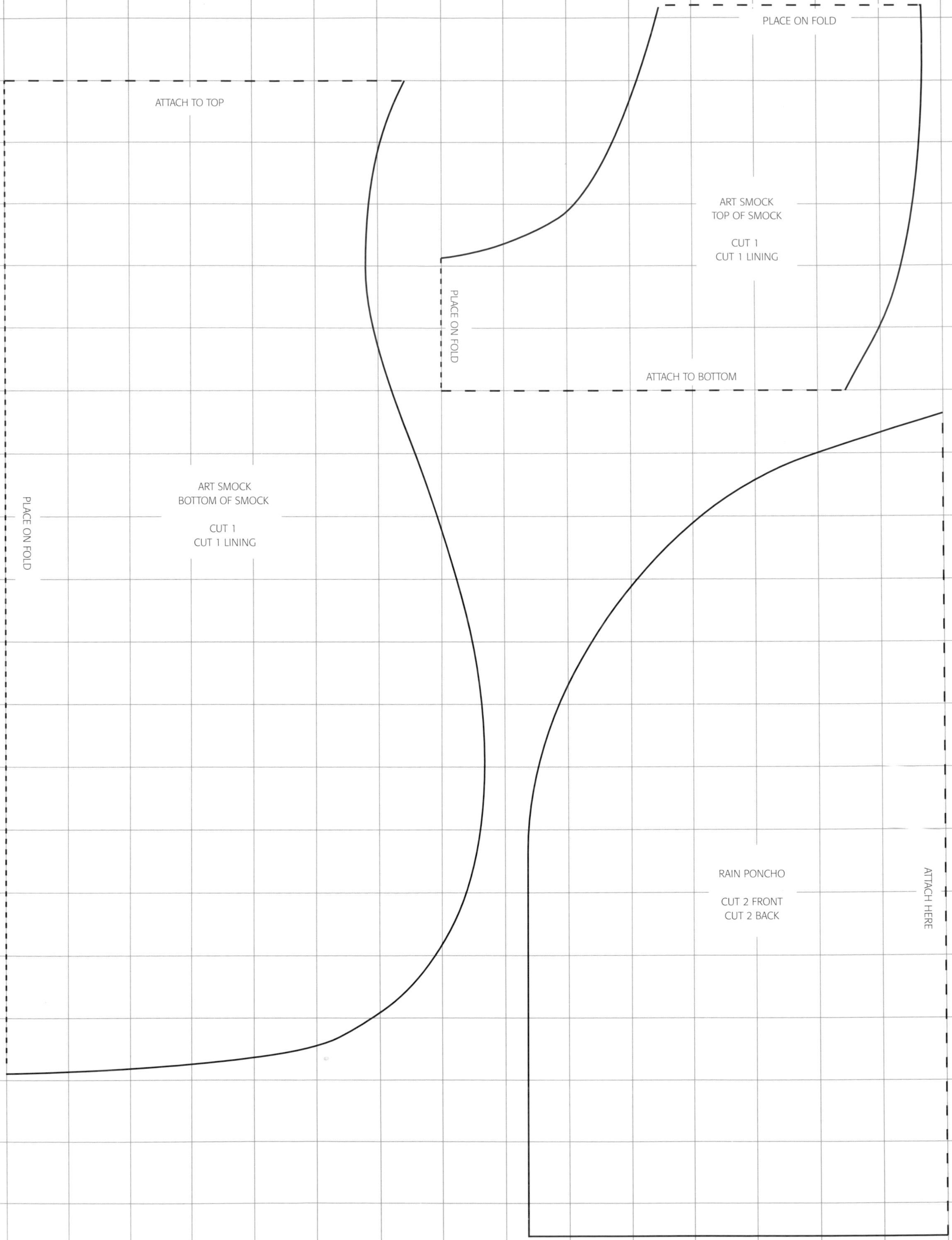

PLACE ON FOLD

ATTACH TO TOP

ART SMOCK
TOP OF SMOCK

CUT 1
CUT 1 LINING

PLACE ON FOLD

ATTACH TO BOTTOM

PLACE ON FOLD

ART SMOCK
BOTTOM OF SMOCK

CUT 1
CUT 1 LINING

RAIN PONCHO

CUT 2 FRONT
CUT 2 BACK

ATTACH HERE

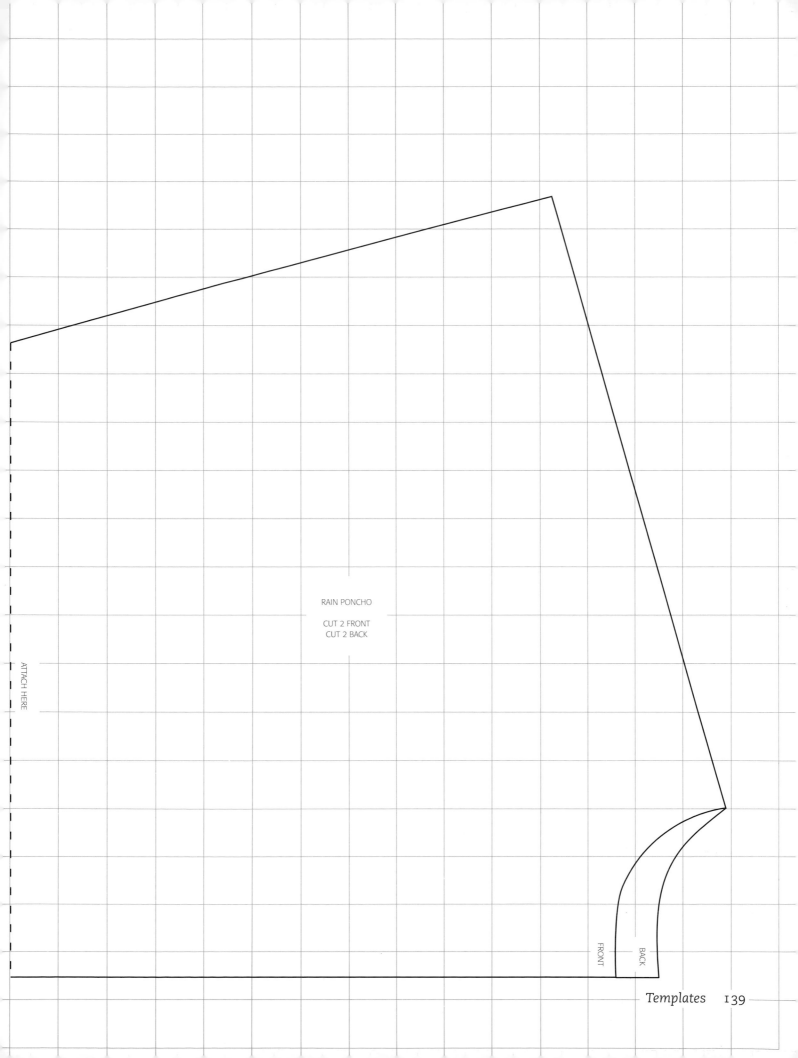

ATTACH HERE

RAIN PONCHO

CUT 2 FRONT
CUT 2 BACK

FRONT

BACK

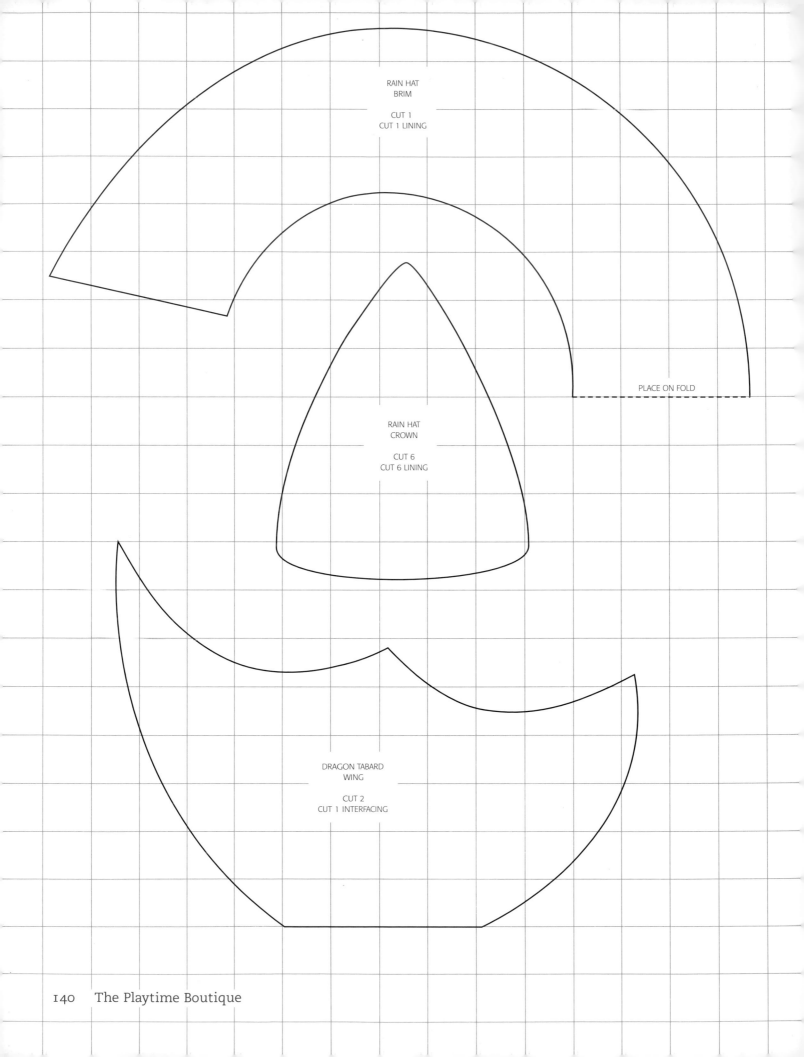

RAIN HAT
BRIM

CUT 1
CUT 1 LINING

RAIN HAT
CROWN

CUT 6
CUT 6 LINING

PLACE ON FOLD

DRAGON TABARD
WING

CUT 2
CUT 1 INTERFACING

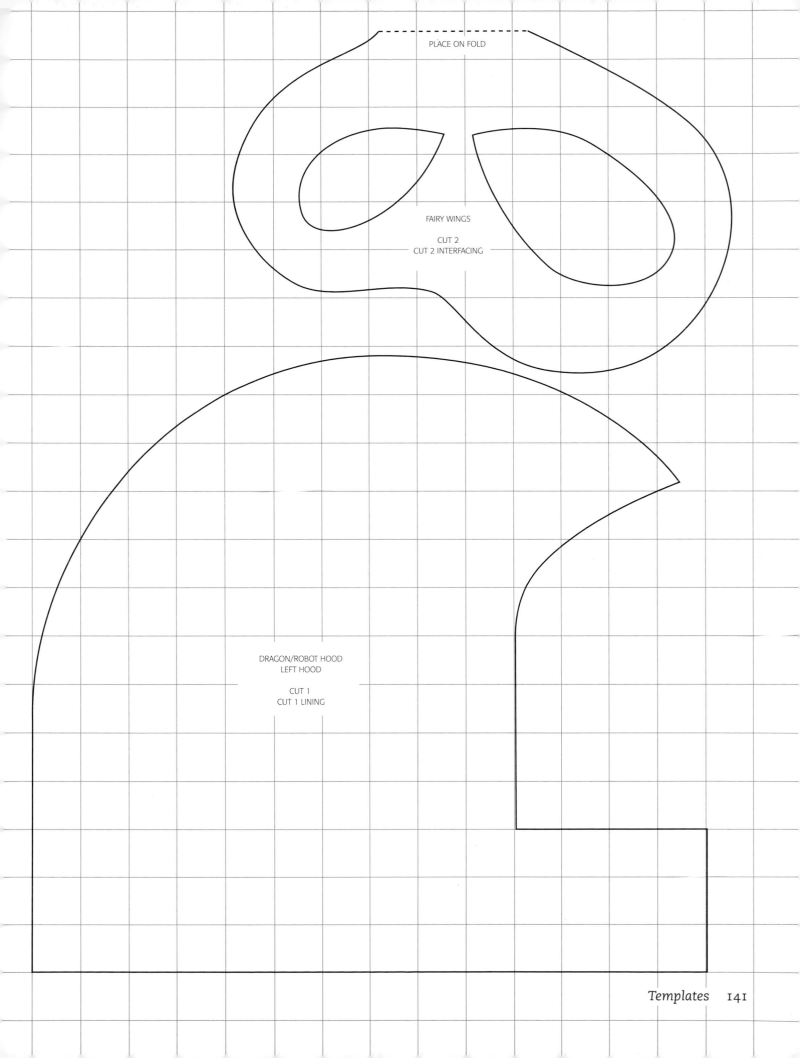

PLACE ON FOLD

FAIRY WINGS

CUT 2
CUT 2 INTERFACING

DRAGON/ROBOT HOOD
LEFT HOOD

CUT 1
CUT 1 LINING

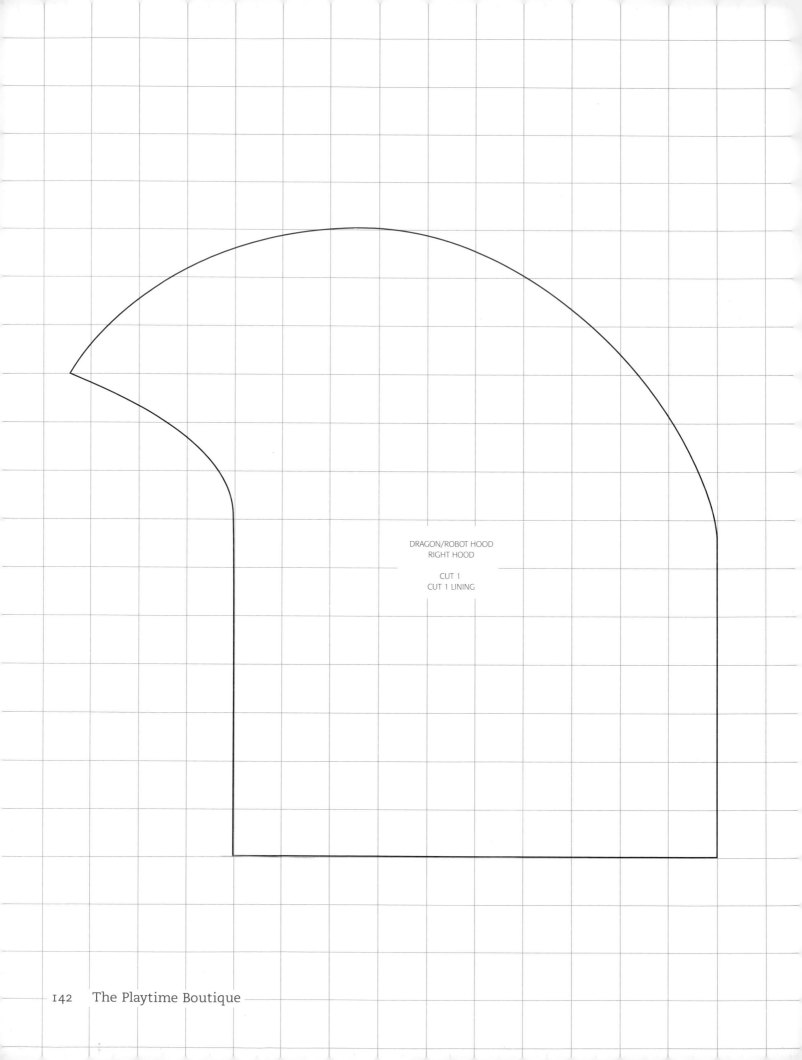

DRAGON/ROBOT HOOD
RIGHT HOOD

CUT 1
CUT 1 LINING

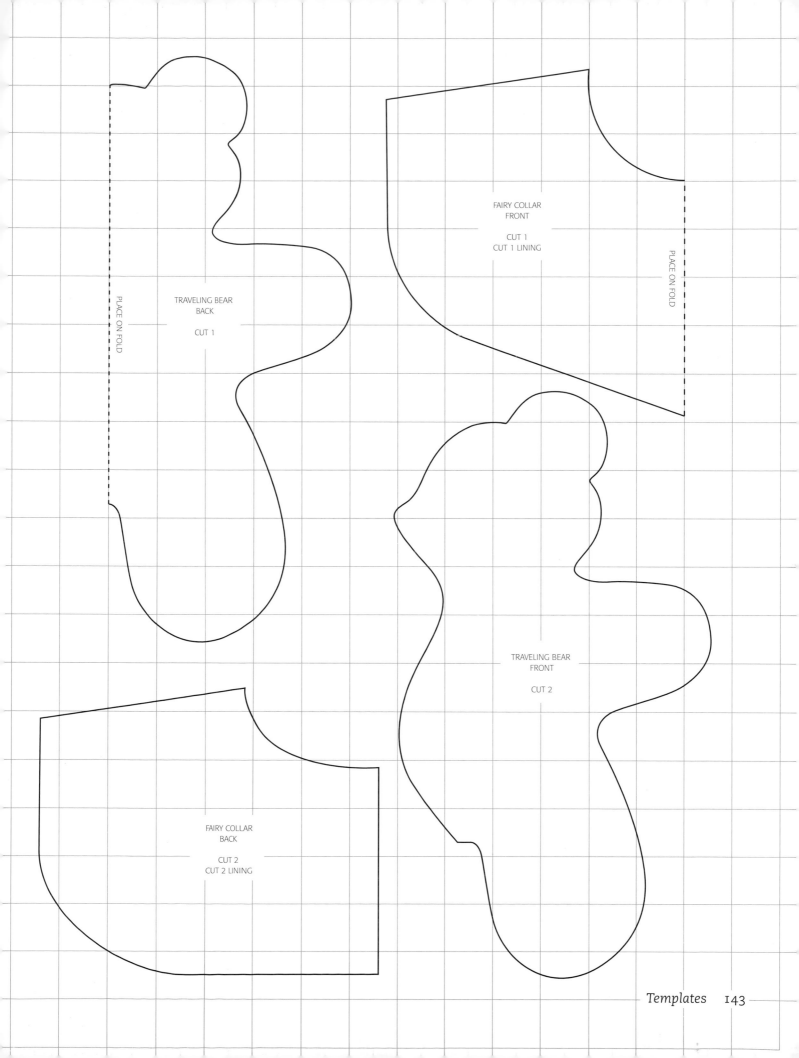

PLACE ON FOLD

TRAVELING BEAR
BACK

CUT 1

FAIRY COLLAR
FRONT

CUT 1
CUT 1 LINING

PLACE ON FOLD

TRAVELING BEAR
FRONT

CUT 2

FAIRY COLLAR
BACK

CUT 2
CUT 2 LINING

FULL-SIZE TEMPLATES;

DO NOT ENLARGE

PLACE ON FOLD

REVERSIBLE TABARD/GAUNTLETS
FLAME

CUT 1

PLACE ON FOLD

REVERSIBLE TABARD/GAUNTLETS
EMBLEM

CUT 1 FOR TABARD
CUT 2 FOR GAUNTLETS

FULL-SIZE TEMPLATES;

DO NOT ENLARGE

TOOTH FAIRY
WINGS

CUT 1

TOOTH FAIRY
APRON

CUT 1

TOOTH FAIRY
DRESS

CUT 1

NUMBER BANNER

CUT 6

NUMBER BANNER

CUT 7

NUMBER BANNER

CUT 9

NUMBER BANNER

CUT 4

NUMBER BANNER

CUT 3

NUMBER BANNER

CUT 2

NUMBER BANNER

CUT 10

NUMBER BANNER

CUT 1

NUMBER BANNER

CUT 8

NUMBER BANNER

CUT 5

TO ENLARGE FOR:		FINISHED HEIGHT
STOP SIGN PILLOW X 150%	(½" : 1½")	3⅜"
GIRL WINDOW VALENCE (CASTLE) X 350%	(½" : 3½")	7⅞"

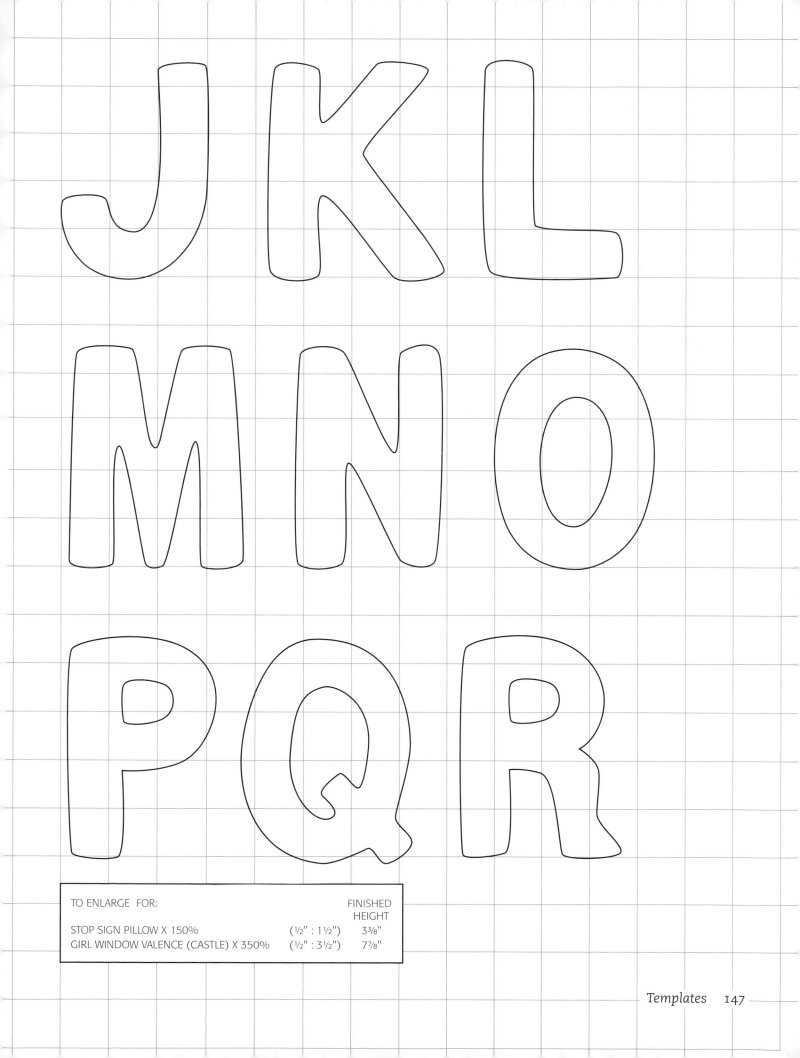

TO ENLARGE FOR:		FINISHED HEIGHT
STOP SIGN PILLOW X 150%	(½" : 1½")	3⅜"
GIRL WINDOW VALENCE (CASTLE) X 350%	(½" : 3½")	7⅞"

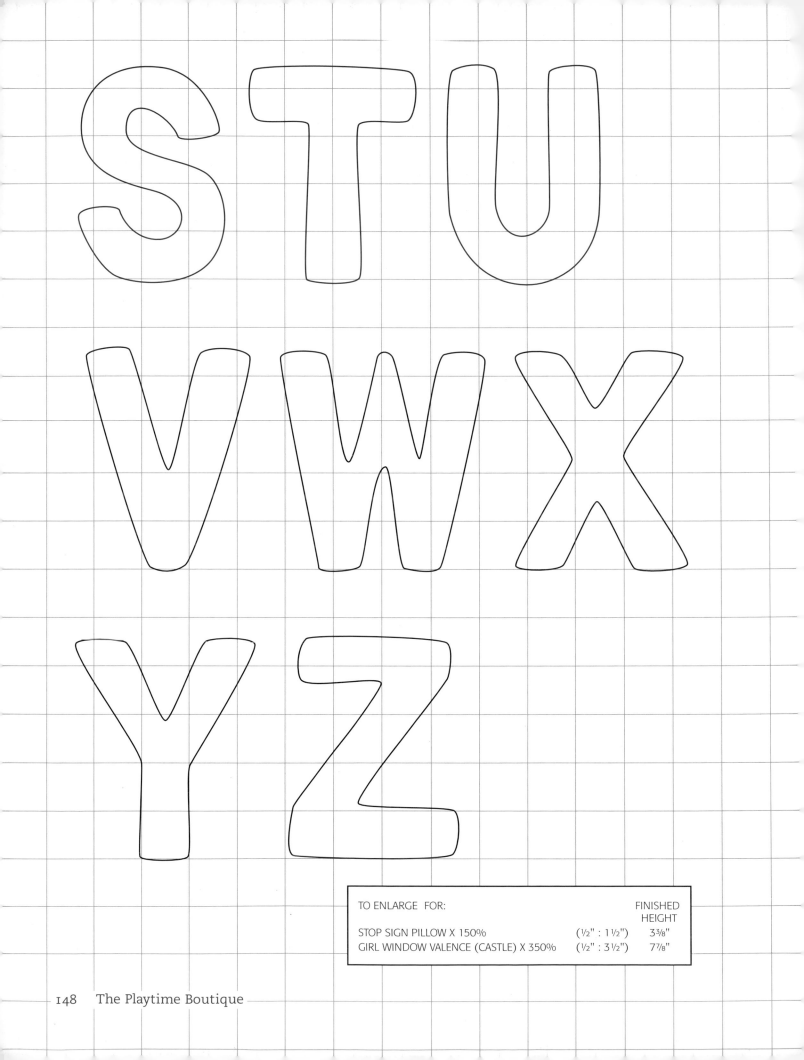

TO ENLARGE FOR:		FINISHED HEIGHT
STOP SIGN PILLOW X 150%	(½" : 1½")	3⅜"
GIRL WINDOW VALENCE (CASTLE) X 350%	(½" : 3½")	7⅞"

TO ENLARGE FOR:		FINISHED HEIGHT
STOP SIGN PILLOW X 150%	(½" : 1½")	3⅜"
GIRL WINDOW VALENCE (CASTLE) X 350%	(½" : 3½")	7⅞"